Lecture Notes in Business Information Processing 544

Series Editors

LNBIP reports state-of-the-art results in areas related to business information systems and industrial application software development – timely, at a high level, and in both printed and electronic form.

The type of material published includes

- Proceedings (published in time for the respective event)
- Postproceedings (consisting of thoroughly revised and/or extended final papers)
- Other edited monographs (such as, for example, project reports or invited volumes)
- Tutorials (coherently integrated collections of lectures given at advanced courses, seminars, schools, etc.)
- Award-winning or exceptional theses

LNBIP is abstracted/indexed in DBLP, EI and Scopus. LNBIP volumes are also submitted for the inclusion in ISI Proceedings.

Jannik Fischbach · Rudolf Ramler ·
Dietmar Winkler · Johannes Bergsmann
Editors

Balancing Software Innovation and Regulatory Compliance

17th International Conference on Software Quality, SWQD 2025
Munich, Germany, May 20–22, 2025
Proceedings

Springer

Editors
Jannik Fischbach
fortiss GmbH
Munich, Germany

Dietmar Winkler
Center for Digital Production (CDP) GmbH & TU Wien
Vienna, Austria

Rudolf Ramler
Software Competence Center Hagenberg GmbH
Hagenberg, Austria

Johannes Bergsmann
Software Quality Lab GmbH
Linz, Austria

ISSN 1865-1348 ISSN 1865-1356 (electronic)
Lecture Notes in Business Information Processing
ISBN 978-3-031-89276-9 ISBN 978-3-031-89277-6 (eBook)
https://doi.org/10.1007/978-3-031-89277-6

This Springer imprint is published by the registered company Springer Nature Switzerland AG
The registered company address is: Gewerbestrasse 11, 6330 Cham, Switzerland

Message from the General Chair

The *Software Quality Days* (SWQD) conference and tools fair was first organized in 2009 and has since grown to become Europe's largest annual industry-oriented conference on software quality, with a strong and vibrant community. The program of the SWQD conference was designed to encompass a stimulating mix of practice-oriented presentations, scientific presentations of new research topics, tutorials, and an exhibition area for tool vendors in the software quality field.

This professional symposium and conference offered a range of valuable opportunities for professional development, new ideas, and networking. Attendees benefited from a series of keynote speeches, professional lectures, exhibits, and tutorials.

The SWQD conference welcomes all who are interested in the wide range of topics related to software quality: software process and quality managers, software testers, test managers, product managers, agile masters, project managers, software architects, software designers, requirements engineers, user interface designers, software developers, IT managers, release managers, development managers, application engineers, DevOps experts, and many more.

The guiding conference topic of SWQD 2025 was *"Software Quality. Balancing Software Innovation and Regulatory Compliance"*, as changed product, process, and service requirements, e.g., distributed engineering projects, mobile applications, involvement of heterogeneous disciplines and stakeholders, extended application areas, and new technologies include new challenges and might require new and adapted methods and tools to master the constantly increasing needs and expectations for quality and security in software systems and applications.

May 2025

Johannes Bergsmann

Message from the Scientific Program Chairs

The 17th *Software Quality Days* (SWQD) conference and tools fair brought together researchers and practitioners from business, industry, and academia working on quality assurance and quality management for software engineering and information technology. The SWQD conference is one of the largest software quality conferences in Europe. SWQD 2025 was organized by fortiss GmbH (Munich, Germany), Software Competence Center Hagenberg GmbH (Hagenberg, Austria), Center for Digital Production GmbH (Vienna, Austria), TU Wien, Institute of Information Systems Engineering (Vienna, Austria), and Software Quality Lab GmbH (Linz, Austria).

Over the past years, we received a growing number of scientific contributions to the SWQD symposium. Starting back in 2012, the SWQD symposium included a dedicated scientific program published in scientific proceedings. In this edition, we received an overall number of 14 high-quality submissions from researchers across the entire globe, which were each peer-reviewed by 4 or more reviewers. Out of these submissions, we selected 4 contributions as full papers, yielding an acceptance rate of 29%. Further, we accepted 2 short papers representing promising research directions to spark discussions between researchers and practitioners on promising work in progress. Finally, we included an invited keynote paper by Jan Bosch and Helena Holmström-Olsson on a critical discussion of digitalization and its impact on organizations. The main topics from academia and industry focused on Model-Based Testing, Software Testing, Machine Learning and Large Language Models, Security and Compliance, and Academic-Industry Collaborations.

To support dissemination and collaboration with practitioners, scientific presentations were integrated into topic-oriented practical tracks. This book is structured according to topics following the guiding conference topic "*Software Quality. Balancing Software Innovation and Regulatory Compliance*":

- Model-Based Software Testing
- Machine Learning and Large Language Models
- Security and Compliance
- Academic-Industry Collaborations.

May 2025

Jannik Fischbach
Rudolf Ramler
Dietmar Winkler

Organization

Organizing Committee

General Chair

Johannes Bergsmann	Software Quality Lab GmbH, Austria

Scientific Program Co-chairs

Jannik Fischbach	fortiss GmbH, Germany
Rudolf Ramler	Software Competence Center Hagenberg GmbH, Austria
Dietmar Winkler	Austrian Center for Digital Production GmbH and TU Wien, Austria

Proceedings Chair

Dietmar Winkler	Austrian Center for Digital Production GmbH and TU Wien, Austria

Organizing and Publicity Chair

Petra Bergsmann	Software Quality Lab GmbH, Austria

Program Committee

Silvia Bonfanti	University of Bergamo, Italy
Matthias Book	University of Iceland, Iceland
Oscar Dieste	Universidad Politécnica de Madrid, Spain
Michael Felderer	German Aerospace Center (DLR), Germany
Henning Femmer	South Westphalia University of Applied Sciences, Germany
Stefan Fischer	Software Competence Center Hagenberg GmbH, Austria
Gordon Fraser	University of Passau, Germany
Julian Frattini	Blekinge Institute of Technology, Sweden

Roman Haas	CQSE GmbH, Germany
Philipp Haindl	St. Pölten University of Applied Sciences, Austria
Jens Heidrich	Fraunhofer IESE, Germany
Eckehard Hermann	University of Applied Sciences Upper Austria, Austria
Frank Houdek	Daimler AG, Germany
Andrea Janes	Free University of Bozen-Bolzano, Italy
Marco Kuhrmann	Reutlingen University, Germany
Harald Lampesberger	University of Applied Sciences Upper Austria, Austria
Christian Macho	University of Klagenfurt, Austria
Eda Marchetti	ISTI-CNR, Italy
Paula Monteiro	University of Minho, Portugal
Dietmar Pfahl	University of Tartu, Estonia
Josef Pichler	University of Applied Sciences Upper Austria, Austria
Rick Rabiser	Johannes Kepler University Linz, Austria
Simon Tjoa	St. Pölten University of Applied Sciences, Austria
Rini Van Solingen	Delft University of Technology, The Netherlands
Daniel Varro	Linköping University, Sweden/McGill University, Canada
Andreas Vogelsang	University of Cologne, Germany

Additional Reviewers

Alexander Stummer
Leopoldo Silva

Contents

Academic-Industry Collaborations

Keynote

Why Digitalization Will Kill Your Company Too

Jan Bosch[1,2(✉)] and Helena Holmström-Olsson[3]

[1] Chalmers University of Technology, Gothenburg, Sweden
jan.bosch@chalmers.se
[2] Eindhoven University of Technology, Eindhoven, The Netherlands
[3] Malmö University, Malmö, Sweden
helena.holmstrom.olsson@mau.se

Abstract. Digitalization is perhaps the primary and most impactful development affecting industry and society. Digitalization is enabled by the digital technologies, i.e., software, data, and artificial intelligence (AI). Many companies digitalize in a slow, iterative fashion by incrementally adding new digital capabilities for individual activities and tasks in an ad-hoc and opportunistic fashion. This increases the risk of disruption. In this paper, we discuss the key challenges companies experience as part of their digital transformation and present the Radical paradigm that can play the role of a North Star for companies to align their change initiatives with. Radical is concerned with being responsive, architecture and data driven, continuous and driven by highly autonomous cross-functional teams and based on three principles, i.e., the three circles model, AI at the core and quantitative outcomes.

Keywords: Digitalization · software-intensive systems · Radical

1 Introduction

Digitalization is perhaps the primary and most impactful development affecting industry and society. Digitalization is enabled by the digital technologies, i.e. software, data and artificial intelligence (AI). Although many view digitalization as a technical challenge, the essence of digitalization is a fundamental shift in value delivery to customers. Whereas value delivery traditionally was transactional, digitalization causes a shift towards continuous value delivery. This is accomplished by frequent software deployments, fast data-driven feedback loops and offline and online training of machine learning models and AI agents.

Frequent software deployments, often referred to as DevOps, have for many years been the norm in software-as-a-service (SaaS) companies, but are increasingly adopted in the software-intensive systems industry. For example, in telecommunications, companies offer new software for telecom equipment every two to four weeks for any customer who wants it.

With the increased connectivity of software-intensive systems, companies are collecting large amounts of data from their products in the field. Initially, this

J. Fischbach et al. (Eds.): SWQD 2025, LNBIP 544, pp. 3–14, 2025.
https://doi.org/10.1007/978-3-031-89277-6_1

data is predominantly used for diagnostics and quality assurance, but over time data providing insight into product performance as well as data used for providing services is increasingly used by companies. One of the core use cases for data is the fast feedback loop in development where the organization can measure the impact of the latest release on the delivered customer value.

AI and specifically machine- and deep-learning (ML/DL) models have become increasingly powerful and have been deployed in various products. More recently, however, AI agents, based on large language models and large multi-model models, have emerged as a revolutionary technology that is expected to affect all industries as well as society at large. AI agents allow us to automate tasks that were not feasible to automate earlier and provide support to professionals that allows for significant productivity improvements.

Although the discussion of the aforementioned technologies may suggest otherwise, the impact of digitalization affects the entire company and not just software R&D. Transitioning from transactional to continuous value delivery, moving from opinions to data and from human effort to AI agents affects, among others, systems engineering, verification and validation, customers support, sales and the general business model underlying the company. Successfully moving through this transition requires a complex, company-wide, highly coordinated change management journey, which many companies struggle with to realize.

To mitigate risk, companies often seek to combine both transactional and continuous revenue streams with the intent of gradually shifting to the latter. The challenge of this approach is that it requires the company to bifurcate all its functions and processes into two categories, i.e. the transactional, slow and waterfall style category and the continuous and fast category. The interface between the functions and processes in both categories tends to be complicated and often leads to conflicts and tensions as both categories optimize for different KPIs.

One confounding factor, especially in Europe, is the increasing regulatory pressure. Many are aware of new regulations such as the Data Act, the AI act, the Product Liability Act and the Cyber Resilience Act, which have potentially quite significant impact on how companies act. However, few realize that companies are already subject to hundreds of regulations. One automotive company claims that they need to comply with somewhere between 250 and 300 regulations and acts. This obviously provides major overhead for companies and tends to cause risk-aversive behavior, slowing down innovation.

So, on the one hand, digitalization requires a significant increase in innovation to ensure that the new capabilities are incorporated sufficiently quickly and companies avoid disruption. On the other hand, the regulatory environment and general organizational resistance to change causes a strong tendency to avoid innovation and unnecessary risks. The result is a situation where companies focus on incremental innovation and avoid more radical innovations.

In this article, we take an alternative standpoint: we present a Radical approach that addresses digitalization in a disruptive fashion. This provides a North Star for companies and provides an alternative paradigm to reason about organizations, value delivery and innovation. This approach consists of three main elements, i.e. the three circles model, AI at the core and quantitative outcomes.

The remainder of the paper is organized as follows. In the next section, we discuss the empirical basis of our research and the main challenges that we have identified. Subsequently, we present our Radical approach. Finally, we conclude the paper in Sect. 4.

2 Empirical Data and Challenges

During the last 14 years, we have had the opportunity to work in close collaboration with the Software Center member companies (www.software-center.se). Software Center is a large research collaboration in which 15 global companies and five Swedish universities work together on topics related to digitalization and digital transformation. The member companies are large software-intensive embedded systems companies operating in domains such as telecommunications, automotive, manufacturing, security, and surveillance. Together, we explore how the companies develop, deploy, and continuously improve software-intensive products and systems with the overall mission of improving the digitalization capabilities in the companies. Our research is qualitative and empirical in nature and we used a case study research approach [16] with workshops and interviews as our primary techniques for data collection. In addition, we engaged in seminars and in different types of company events to further strengthen our relationship to the companies and to learn even more about the opportunities and challenges they face in their development, deployment and improvement of software-intensive embedded systems. Our research spans over more than a decade and during this time we have reported on, e.g., the adoption and evolution of software development practices and processes [2,3], feature experimentation and data-driven development practices [9,10,19,20], the adoption and use of DevOps, DataOps and MLOps [2,6,12,17], digitalization and digital transformation [5,23], and innovation opportunities and new business models [24] to name a few of the topics we studied.

In addition to the member companies in Software Center, we worked with several additional companies in the software-as-a-service (SaaS) domain with the main reason being that these companies are often more advanced in using digital technologies such as software, data, and artificial intelligence (AI). Hence, we studied these companies to gain insights and learn about best practices to then transfer these to the embedded systems domain and the companies in Software Center.

Our research shows that all companies are driving improvements and they are adopting digital technologies to enhance already existing products as well as develop entirely new products. However, progress is slow and the adoption of new ways-of-working is not as effective as what is desired to not run the risk of being disrupted. Although data and AI technologies are increasingly important and already critical components in most of the systems we studied, the companies face huge challenges with respect to digitalization and how to rapidly transform their business to stay competitive.

Below, we present a summary and generalization of the *key challenges* companies face with respect to digitalization. These challenges work as the basis for our discussion on RADICAL as a new paradigm to help companies reinvent the practices they use with the intent to increase responsiveness, improve value delivery and advance their digital capabilities.

- All companies we studied have adopted *agile practices* and refer to these as the primary approach to software development. However, while agile practices have helped the companies to shorten development lead time, we note how there is an increasing focus on the 'how' rather than on the 'why' and the 'what' of development. As a result, many companies have become process-driven and they have lost sight of the outcomes they seek to achieve. As noted already in 2014, more than half of all the features in a typical software system are never used by customers and hence, the development of these is a waste of resources that could have been allocated elsewhere [1]. In our experience, the challenge with agile practices is a too strong feature focus and a too vague idea of what adds value to customers. Despite more than two decades of applying agile ways-of-working, many companies still struggle with how to continuously improve and validate new functionality. Although feature development is rapid there are few mechanisms to help determine if a feature adds value to customers. In the companies we studied, this had lead to an increasing push-back on agile practices as people feel it doesn't support the reality of today's product development [4].
- To be able to work in an agile fashion, there is the need for *short feedback cycles*. However, many of the companies we studied experience the opposite in that there is a lack of short feedback cycles. This situation makes incremental and iterative development difficult as there are no effective mechanisms for frequent deployment and rapid feedback from customers. Even if several companies deploy on a frequent basis, and are able to push software functionality to customers on a very regular basis, they struggle with making effective use of the data coming back from the field and that could provide good insights on the usage of features. Agile development, and the opportunity to benefit from data-driven practices, assume short feedback cycles. However, this is not the reality for most companies in the B2B industry. Several of the companies we studied build highly complex products with limited opportunities to validate with customers. Typically, there is no direct access to the end-user and therefore, valuable feedback on feature usage and customer value is difficult to obtain.
- For fast feedback loops to work in practice, and to benefit from these, companies need to have *continuous practices* in place [2]. This implies having the infrastructure and process for continuous integration (CI) and continuous delivery and deployment (CD) [6,19]. Although most people appreciate the idea of continuous practices, i.e., continuous development, delivery, deployment and improvement of software features, data and ML/DL models, they

tend to rather adopt a "perfectionist mind-set" meaning that most engineers take pride in developing and deploying the complete system to customers rather than thinking in terms of smaller increments, an MVP style to development [13] and using an approach where systems grow over time rather than being complete from the start. This engineering culture make anything except traditional waterfall development very difficult. Despite having sophisticated technical infrastructures for enabling continuous practices, people still find it hard to understand why customers would appreciate anything less than a complete system that is fully functional. This reflects a big gap between what continuous practices emphasize and what happens in practice.

- To benefit from continuous practices, and to be able to monetize on new and frequently added functionality, companies need to shift their business model from *transactional to continuous business models.* This however, has proven to be very difficult. The companies we studied are product-centric companies and have employed transactional business models where they get paid at the time of sale. As most companies align their revenue and cost models, there is often resistance towards using a DevOps approach [7] as this would imply continuous cost for creating each release, but no recurring revenue. Based on our experience, most companies are experimenting with continuous business models, but a common challenge is that it is difficult to convince a customer to pay for additional functionality, i.e., new services, when having paid upfront for the product.
- While struggling with the adoption of continuous business models, the increasing number of *new regulations and laws* makes it even more difficult for companies to accelerate and strive in a digitalized world. In all companies we worked with, the many recent regulations and laws, e.g., Data Act, AI Act, GDPR, Product Liability Act, Cybersecurity Act, Cyber Resilience Act, impose major challenges for developing software, data and AI-intensive systems. Depending on the industry, certification is done by external certification authorities or companies can self-certify, but there is often a significant cost associated with certification. Part of the challenge is that regulatory authorities assume a waterfall development and validation approach and hence, certification tends to be a significant undertaking. Although iterative approaches for certification exist, e.g. SafeScrum [11], these approaches have not yet reached the maturity stage needed for deployment. As a consequence of this, the adoption of DevOps and MLOps practices becomes difficult if not impossible and many companies experience a situation in which critical resources are spent on regulatory compliance rather than product improvements and innovation.
- Finally, as an overarching challenge, all companies struggle with how to effectively develop, evolve and manage *data and AI technologies.* Although data-driven practices are not new, and although AI engineering practices exist, the development, integration and continuous evolution of data and AI components is difficult. In our previous research, we studied data management practices [17,18], data-driven development practices [8–10], ML/DL model development and deployment [12] and engineering of AI-enhanced systems

[14,15]. Our research captures the many challenges that companies experience and the solutions that exist. What we see is that AI, and specifically machine- and deep-learning (ML/DL) models, have become increasingly powerful and have been deployed in various products. However, the pace in which digital technologies are adopted, and the associated practices that companies need to manage these, is slow. Transitioning from transactional to continuous value delivery, moving from opinions to data and from human effort to AI agents affects all functions and all roles in a company. Successfully moving through this transition requires a complex, company-wide, highly coordinated change management journey, which we so far haven't seen in practice.

3 RADICAL Paradigm

Digitalization enabled by software, data and AI, is disrupting industries and companies. Many seek to respond in a slow, iterative fashion by incrementally adding new digital capabilities for individual activities and tasks. Although this certainly leads to improvements and better outcomes, the fact that a company is better today than yesterday is not sufficient to protect it from disruption. It may well be that competitors and new entrants take a more disruptive approach that allows them to harvest the benefits more rapidly and, through that, disrupt your company.

Our experience with a variety of companies is that the changes towards digitalization tend to be opportunistic and more driven by where there is a path of least resistance rather than moving towards a North Star or desired state that provides strategic guidance and direction. In this section, we present an approach that in our view can play the role of a North Star for companies to align their change initiatives with.

The approach we propose is called Radical. Radical is an acronym that captures the essence of what in our view constitutes the next paradigm that for product-centric companies after the Agile paradigm. The acronym can be summarized as follows:

- **Responsive**: Whereas agile is a reactive methodology, product development needs a clear sense of direction and strategy. We are responsive to external influences, but not controlled by these.
- **Architecture**: Whereas agile prioritizes human interaction, the result is coordination through meetings. Using architectural interfaces to decouple different teams is a much more efficient approach through coordination.
- **Data-driven**: Although companies tend to collect vast amounts of data, most decisions in companies are still opinion-based. We need to adopt data-driven decision making and follow the adage of Edwards Deming: In God we trust. All others must bring data.
- **Integrated cross-functional alignment**: Rather than relying on inter-team or inter-function coordination between product management, systems engineering, software R&D and other functions, organize cross-functional teams where all skills necessary for a task or project are in the same team.

- **Continuous**: In the age of DevOps, we need to stop thinking in terms of projects with a clear start and end. Instead, we adopt a continuous way of working where we iterate and use the data from the last iteration to inform the work of this one.
- **Aligned on business goals**: Despite all the bluster to the contrary, very few companies are aligned on business goals and many focus on local optimization serving their team or function. Using clearly defined quantitative outcomes, the entire organization needs to aligned on these and each individual and team measured on their contribution to these outcomes.
- **Leadership**: Although leadership is a highly overloaded and abused term, we need leaders that set the right organizational culture, defined and communicate purpose and manage conflicts in the organization.

We have discussed the elements of Radical in an earlier paper [4] and refer to the reader to that. In this paper, we focus on three key principles underlying Radical, i.e. the three circles model, AI at the core and quantitative outcomes.

3.1 Three Circles Model

In a digital business, all core business processes are to the highest extent automated and controlled in an automated fashion using quantitative performance data. In fact, we can conceptualize a digital business as consisting of three circles of activities (see Fig. 1).

The most inner circle consists of the core value delivery business processes of the company. For instance, for an e-commerce website, this includes the presentation of items, recommendations, managing orders, taking payments, etc. These activities typically have no or very limited human involvement and are completely automated. In the case that core value delivery processes can not be automated fully, such as warehouse tasks, the humans tend to be instrumented with data collection and subject to the same quantitative performance management as the automated parts of the process. The first circle is concerned with operations and activities that support operations.

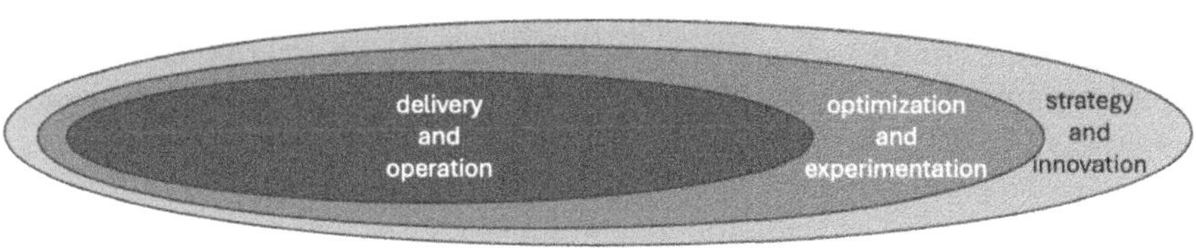

Fig. 1. Three Circles Model

The second circle of activity involves human actors and, more recently, potentially even AI agents, who use quantitative data for analytics and experimentation. The main focus of this circle is to instrument the core business processes in the inner circle and to tune and optimize these. In this case, for instance, analytics may show that items that are recommended to customers by the recommendation engine are selected and bought in 0.15% of the cases. As the industry average is higher than that, one of the activities in this circle might then be to experiment with different recommendation algorithms using A/B testing to evaluate whether the success rate of the recommendation engine can be improved to match the industry average.

The second circle is concerned with tactics and activities that improve the performance of the operational core. It is important to note that activities in this circle do not have to be performed by humans. It is entirely feasible, for instance, to have a system run autonomous improvement activities that focus on optimizing the core business processes.

Finally, the third circle is concerned with those business activities that are strategic in nature. As strategic activities tend to be concerned with interpreting trends and predicting the future, it tends to be challenging to quantify these. Characteristic for activities in this circle is that the focus tends to be on the purpose of the business, the role it plays in its ecosystem and the way it seeks to differentiate and complement itself towards others. Although AI agents do play a role here, for instance for processing large amounts of external information, this circle is driven primarily by humans.

The three circles of activities are different from each other not just in terms of automation and use of data, but also in the cycle time and speed at which each circle operates. The operations circle runs, by its very nature, in seconds, minutes and hours. The tactical circle operates in days and weeks whereas the strategic circle tends to operate in months and years.

It is helpful to think about companies in three distinct circles of activity, i.e. delivery and operations, optimization and experimentation and, finally, strategy and innovation, that have completely different characteristics, cycle times and success metrics. Our empirical data shows that many tend to mix up the activities in the different circles, which tends to lead to confusion and sub-par performance.

3.2 AI at the Core

Our experience with the companies that we work with is that these companies use new AI capabilities in a relatively ad-hoc, opportunistic and focused on smaller, complementing activities. Although this leads to smaller improvements, these approaches fail to capitalize on the full potential of using AI in organizations.

AI is so promising as it allows us to automate tasks and activities that were impossible to automate earlier. However, there are often additional reasons why automation failed in earlier stages and that can only be partially solved by AI. A typical reason is that we have allowed too much variation and human interpretation in a process or workflow rather than standardizing the process or workflow. If too much human interpretation is required to execute, then also AI will not be able to automate without vast amounts of training data to cover all the human-driven variations.

To be able to capitalize the full potential that AI provides to companies, especially the most inner delivery and operations circle needs to be redesigned from scratch based on the principle of "AI at the core". All activities in the inner circle need to, by default, be designed to be executed fully automated using traditional means or using AI agents. Only where we are unable to automate tasks are humans brought in, but these humans work "below the algorithm" and are basically instructed what to do by the system and instrumented and closely measured to ensure compliance and minimal variation in performance.

The redesign of the core value delivery processes and workflows follows a series of steps:

- **Identify key workflows**: The first step in this process is to identify the key workflows that are concerned with value delivery to customers. Especially in older companies, this tends to be a rather confusing as these processes have evolved for decades and contain all kinds of exceptions, special cases and variations that it tends to be difficult to get clear answers on what these workflows are. Our experience is that different roles often have quite different views and perspectives and these need to be harmonized as part of the process.
- **Define KPIs for each workflow**: Once the workflows are defined, we need, for each workflow, to define KPIs to quantitatively define either the value to the customer or to the company. These KPIs can then be used to drive improvement.
- **Standardize each workflow**: As the identified workflows have often evolved for a long time, we need to standardize the workflow to the largest extent possible. Each exception and special case needs to be reviewed and decided upon. Whereas is preferable to remove as much variation as possible, the workflow can contain these if the rules are clear and quantified. An alternative is to define additional workflows.
- **Develop automation for each workflow**: Once the workflow is simplified and more standardized, often traditional algorithmic and rule-based automation can more easily be developed. Rather than using AI as a silver bullet, it often is preferable to use traditional approaches where feasible. Standardizing workflows tends to allow for automation in places where it was not feasible before.
- **Identify problematic areas and develop AI agents**: Where traditional automation is not feasible, the next step is to experiment with AI agents to solve the task at hand. This often requires cases and training data to contextualize generic AI models.
- **For any remaining action, define human roles and tasks**: The intent is to break each workflow into tasks and seek to automate each task using traditional automation or AI agents. Where that proves to be infeasible, the task falls to humans. However, these activities are "below the algorithm" and should be highly standardized, instrumented and measured.

Due to the length of the paper, we can only discuss this principle at a high level, but there is much more available as reinventing the core value delivery processes and workflows in a company proves to be incredibly hard in practice.

3.3 Quantitative Outcomes

During the fourteen years that we have worked with Software Center companies as well as other companies, we have at many occasions worked on quantification of product value, feature value, team performance as well as numerous other aspects of organizations. The surprising realization that we have come to is that most companies, except for financial metrics, largely operate on opinions and qualitative expressions of value.

The challenge is that anything that includes digital technologies requires some form of quantification. As a simple example, if a company decides to run an A/B experiment for one of its features, it needs to defined what "better" looks like as, in the end, a choice needs to be made between alternative A and B. So, if alternative A improves customer satisfaction but reduced revenue and alternative B does the opposite, we need to have a clear quantification and relative prioritization of the two factors to decide whether to roll out A or B.

In SaaS companies, especially in e-commerce, this is often quite easy: conversion is the only metric that matters. Software-intensive embedded systems companies, however, often have a wide variety of variables that they consider to contribute value to customers. Consequently, these companies often fall in the "worthwhile many" trap, meaning that instead of focusing on the "vital few", these companies use dozens upon dozens of variables to measure value. The result of this is twofold. First, as there is no prioritization of these variables, everyone can do whatever they want and have a story on how they deliver value. Second, when the number of prioritized metrics goes beyond a very small number, it provides no guidance any longer to the organization and becomes useless.

In our research, we have worked on value modeling for several years, see e.g. [21,22], but we still experience significant reticence, confusion and lack of interest of the companies that we work with. However, any company that seeks to become more data-driven and use AI in any form is required to explicitly define how the value that it delivers to customers can be measured in quantitative terms.

Value modeling is conducted in a 10 step process including the following steps: Identify key value factors, prioritisation of key value factors, translation of hypothesis into an experiment and conduct experiment. Due to lack of space, we are unable to describe these steps in more detail, but refer to [21,22] for more details.

4 Conclusions and Future Work

Digitalization is perhaps the primary and most impactful development affecting industry and society. Digitalization is enabled by the digital technologies, i.e. software, data and artificial intelligence (AI). Whereas value delivery traditionally was transactional, digitalization causes a shift towards continuous value delivery. This is accomplished by frequent software deployments, fast data-driven feedback loops and offline and online training of machine learning models.

Many companies digitalize in a slow, iterative fashion by incrementally adding new digital capabilities for individual activities and tasks in an ad-hoc and opportunistic fashion. Although this certainly leads to improvements and better outcomes, the fact that a company is better today than yesterday is not sufficient to protect it from disruption.

In this paper, we presented the Radical paradigm that can play the role of a North Star for companies to align their change initiatives with. Radical is concerned with being responsive, architecture and data driven, continuous and driven by highly autonomous cross-functional teams. Three principles underlying Radical, i.e. the three circles model, AI at the core and quantitative outcomes.

In future work, we aim to work with the Software Center companies to realize the Radical paradigm in their respective organizations and to further validate the approach that we presented in this paper.

References

1. Backlund, E., Bolle, M., Tichy, M., Olsson, H.H., Bosch, J.: Automated user interaction analysis for workflow-based web portals. In: Lassenius, C., Smolander, K. (eds.) ICSOB 2014. LNBIP, vol. 182, pp. 148–162. Springer, Cham (2014). https://doi.org/10.1007/978-3-319-08738-2_11
2. Bosch, J.: Continuous software engineering: an introduction. In: Bosch, J. (ed.) Continuous Software Engineering, pp. 3–13. Springer, Cham (2014). https://doi.org/10.1007/978-3-319-11283-1_1
3. Bosch, J.: Speed, data, and ecosystems: the future of software engineering. IEEE Softw. **33**(1), 82–88 (2015)
4. Bosch, J., Holmström Olsson, H.: The end of agile as we know it. Submitted Inter. J. (2025)
5. Bosch, J., Olsson, H.H.: Digital for real: a multicase study on the digital transformation of companies in the embedded systems domain. J. Softw. Evolution Process **33**(5), e2333 (2021)
6. Dakkak, A., Bosch, J., Olsson, H.H., Mattos, D.I.: Continuous deployment in software-intensive system-of-systems. Inf. Softw. Technol. **159**, 107200 (2023)
7. Ebert, C., Gallardo, G., Hernantes, J., Serrano, N.: Devops. IEEE Softw. **33**(3), 94–100 (2016)
8. Fabijan, A., Dmitriev, P., McFarland, C., Vermeer, L., Holmström Olsson, H., Bosch, J.: Experimentation growth: evolving trustworthy a/b testing capabilities in online software companies. J. Softw. Evolut. Process **30**(12), e2113 (2018)
9. Fabijan, A., Dmitriev, P., Olsson, H.H., Bosch, J.: The evolution of continuous experimentation in software product development: from data to a data-driven organization at scale. In: 2017 IEEE/ACM 39th International Conference on Software Engineering (ICSE), pp. 770–780. IEEE (2017)
10. Fabijan, A., Olsson, H.H., Bosch, J.: Data-driven decision-making in product r&d. Springer (2015)
11. Hanssen, G.K., Stålhane, T., Myklebust, T.: SafeScrum®-Agile development of safety-critical software. Springer (2018)
12. John, M.M., Olsson, H.H., Bosch, J.: Towards an ai-driven business development framework: a multi-case study. J. Softw. Evolut. Proc. **35**(6), e2432 (2023)

13. Lenarduzzi, V., Taibi, D.: Mvp explained: a systematic mapping study on the definitions of minimal viable product. In: 2016 42th Euromicro Conference on Software Engineering and Advanced Applications (SEAA), pp. 112–119. IEEE (2016)
14. Lwakatare, L.E., Raj, A., Bosch, J., Olsson, H.H., Crnkovic, I.: A taxonomy of software engineering challenges for machine learning systems: an empirical investigation. In: Kruchten, P., Fraser, S., Coallier, F. (eds.) XP 2019. LNBIP, vol. 355, pp. 227–243. Springer, Cham (2019). https://doi.org/10.1007/978-3-030-19034-7_14
15. Lwakatare, L.E., Raj, A., Crnkovic, I., Bosch, J., Olsson, H.H.: Large-scale machine learning systems in real-world industrial settings: a review of challenges and solutions. Inf. Softw. Technol. **127**, 106368 (2020)
16. Maxwell, J.A.: Qualitative research design: an interactive approach. Sage Publications (2012)
17. Munappy, A.R., Bosch, J., Olsson, H.H., Arpteg, A., Brinne, B.: Data management for production quality deep learning models: challenges and solutions. J. Syst. Softw. **191**, 111359 (2022)
18. Munappy, A.R., Mattos, D.I., Bosch, J., Olsson, H.H., Dakkak, A.: From ad-hoc data analytics to dataops. In: Proceedings of the International Conference on Software and System Processes, pp. 165–174 (2020)
19. Olsson, H.H., Alahyari, H., Bosch, J.: Climbing th "stairway to heaven"–a mulitiple-case study exploring barriers in the transition from agile development towards continuous deployment of software. In: 2012 38th Euromicro Conference on Software Engineering and Advanced Applications, pp. 392–399. IEEE (2012)
20. Olsson, H.H., Bosch, J.: The HYPEX model: from opinions to data-driven software development. In: Bosch, J. (ed.) Continuous Software Engineering, pp. 155–164. Springer, Cham (2014). https://doi.org/10.1007/978-3-319-11283-1_13
21. Olsson, H.H., Bosch, J.: Towards continuous validation of customer value. In: Scientific Workshop Proceedings of the XP2015, pp. 1–4 (2015)
22. Olsson, H.H., Bosch, J.: Make up your mind: towards a comprehensive definition of customer value in large scale software development. CLEI Electr. J. **21**(1) (2018)
23. Olsson, H.H., Bosch, J.: Going digital: disruption and transformation in software-intensive embedded systems ecosystems. J. Softw. Evolut. Proc. **32**(6), e2249 (2020)
24. Olsson, H.H., Bosch, J.: Living in a pink cloud or fighting a whack-a-mole? on the creation of recurring revenue streams in the embedded systems domain. In: 2022 48th Euromicro Conference on Software Engineering and Advanced Applications (SEAA), pp. 161–168. IEEE (2022)

Model-Based Software Testing

Model-Based Test Design in SysML for System Requirements Verification and Validation

Elif Ugur(✉) and Andreas Wübbeke

South Westphalia University of Applied Sciences, 59494 Soest, Germany
elifu98@hotmail.com, elif.ugur@iem.fraunhofer.de,
wuebbeke.andreas@fh-swf.de

Abstract. In this contribution, we introduce a Model-Based Test Design (MBTD) approach that reuses the existing diagram types of Systems Modeling Language (SysML) 1.5 to improve test design quality for larger cyber-physical systems. The approach also facilitates the traceability between requirements and test cases to measure the test coverage and supports the idea of Model-Based Systems Engineering (MBSE). We validated our approach by applying it to a real-world Systems Engineering (SE) project of a cyber-physical system.

Keywords: Model-Based Test Design (MBTD) · Systems Modeling Language (SysML) · Model-Based Systems Engineering (MBSE) · Systems Engineering (SE)

1 Introduction

Systems Engineering (SE), as understood today, is a well-known approach supported by several processes, methods, languages, and tools [1–3]. In our understanding, and also referring to the INCOSE[1] the future of SE is model-based [4]. As the number of cyber-physical systems increases, where mechanical, electrical, electronic, and software have to work together, SE is increasingly becoming the focus in both industry and research.

Model-Based Systems Engineering (MBSE) is currently based primarily on the international standard SysML [5] by the Object Management Group (OMG)[2]. The recently published version 2.0 is not yet widely supported by tools or even used in the industry. Therefore, our contribution focuses on the previous version, SysML 1.5.

The aim of MBSE is to create a common model for modeling complex systems, supported by various views (requirements, structural, and behavioral). This strategy offers several advantages over document-based methods, particularly in terms of consistency, traceability, and readability of the specified system [6, 7].

The designed system model(s) aims to support the entire lifecycle of system development, beginning with requirements gathering, architecture, and detailed design, followed by the implementation of different system aspects. Following the V-Model of SE [8], as

[1] http://incose.org
[2] http://omg.org

J. Fischbach et al. (Eds.): SWQD 2025, LNBIP 544, pp. 17–35, 2025.
https://doi.org/10.1007/978-3-031-89277-6_2

illustrated in [9], the constructive parts of the V-Model (left side) are supported by the corresponding testing levels on the right side. Testing provides an analytical way to ensure the system's quality, with different levels known in the V-Model: Unit/Module Testing, Integration Testing, System Testing, and Acceptance Testing. In this contribution, we focus on the level of System Testing, as the SE also focuses on this level.

To systematically test a system, there are also well-known approaches like [10]. One central aspect, besides other parts of the testing process, is the design of Test Cases based on the defined requirements and system design elements.

As previously mentioned, SE is a model-based domain nowadays; therefore, the test design process should ideally be model-based as well. This contribution aims to connect the existing model-based SE approach with MBTD, thereby reinforcing advantages like consistency, traceability, and readability.

In the next section, we provide further details on the underlying problem as well as the research questions addressed by our contribution.

2 Problem Statement and Research Questions

2.1 Problem Statement

When it comes to testing a system modeled with an MBSE approach using SysML, SysML currently offers very limited support for modeling test assets. The only possibility is to model test cases with titles and textual descriptions in a requirements diagram, where test cases can be linked to requirements using <<verify>> links. In such diagrams, requirements are typically represented as green rectangular blocks, while test cases are modeled in yellow blocks, connected through dashed <<verify>> relationships. This representation (illustrated in Fig. 1, discussed in Subsect. 4.1) highlights the abstract linkage between requirements and test cases but lacks the granularity to incorporate critical test design elements such as pre- and post-conditions, test steps, test data, and expected results [11], all of which are necessary to create executable test cases.

Currently, this must be done using separate test management approaches and tools, primarily document-based. This disconnection of languages and tools leads to several drawbacks concerning the quality assurance of designed systems:

- Ensuring consistency across requirements and test models. Did I test every requirement? Are test cases defined according to the requirements specification?
- Automated measurement of test coverage of requirements is not possible if the tools used for requirements modeling and test modeling lack traceability features.
- Are changes in requirements or test cases synchronized? Do test cases remain up-to-date and properly aligned with the latest system specifications?

2.2 Research Questions and Goals

Based on the problem statement, in this contribution, we want to address the three following research questions:

RQ1: How can we ensure good quality of Testing in MBSE?
RQ1.1: If MBSE today does not include Test Design, how can we interrelate both?

RQ1.2: How can we measure and improve the Quality of Testing based on the interrelation?

RQ1 is the guiding question. Good quality of a test approach depends on several aspects, which of course cannot be holistically addressed by us here. We want to focus on the interaction, consistency, and usability of the requirements and test models. To make this more concrete RQ1.1 deals with the question how to interrelate both models with each other to again foster the idea of a single model in SE.

Furthermore, RQ1.2 adds the question how, based on an interrelated requirements and test model, the quality of the testing can be (automatically) measured and finally be improved.

The remainder of our contribution is structured as follows: In Sect. 3 the provided research questions are discussed with respect to existing related work to show the research gap. Afterward, this gap is addressed by our own solution in Sect. 4. In Sect. 5 we validate our solution based on a qualitative study. The final Sect. 6 summarizes and discusses the results of our contribution and gives an outlook on future research opportunities.

3 Related Work

The integration of MBSE with a model-based approach to test design is essential for addressing the disconnect between system requirements and testing, particularly within the SE V-Model. This section reviews existing literature, identifying key challenges and evaluating methodologies proposed to enhance alignment between requirements and testing phases.

MBSE has become a widely adopted approach for managing the complexity of modern SE projects. According to [12], MBSE significantly improves early project phases such as requirements gathering, architectural design, and traceability by providing a structured framework that effectively integrates system components. Additionally, SysML serves as a central tool in MBSE, offering capabilities to comprehensively model system requirements, behavior, and structure. As highlighted in [12], the adoption of SysML continues to grow due to its ability to create unified models that bridge system development and verification processes.

However, despite these advantages, MBSE and SysML face significant challenges in aligning system requirements with testing processes. [13] emphasizes the disconnect between the left (requirements and design) and right (testing and validation) sides of the V-Model, which often results in incomplete test coverage, late detection of issues, and increased costs due to rework. Similarly, [14] highlights the challenge of detecting emergent behaviors in complex systems, which frequently manifest only in late-stage testing, causing costly delays. In agile environments, [15] points to additional challenges, including maintaining traceability across different levels of abstraction and synchronizing changes between requirements and test models.

One approach to addressing these issues is integrating system requirements and system testing through a model-based test design methodology. [16] demonstrates that defining test cases in a model-based manner supports consistency across integration levels, enhances the reusability of test cases, and reduces overall testing effort. However, [13] shows that current implementations often remain as proofs of concept rather than fully scalable strategies. For example, [17] proposes a two-stage Verification & Validation (V&V) strategy extending SysML's capabilities with external tools for early and continuous testing, but this reliance on external platforms introduces workflow complexity. Similarly, [18] enhances the organization and traceability of test artifacts within SysML but does not comprehensively address the complexities of integrating testing with broader SE processes.

In addition to these methodologies, the UML Testing Profile (UTP), based on the Unified Modeling Language (UML), and the Telling TestStories (TTS) approach represent established contributions in the field of model-based testing. UTP, standardized by OMG, provides a structured framework for defining and documenting test artifacts within UML-based environments [19]. While it standardizes essential testing elements such as Test Objectives and Test Contexts, its reliance on UML makes it less accessible for systems engineers who primarily work with SysML. Similarly, TTS offers a model-driven testing methodology aimed at service-oriented architectures, emphasizing iterative and incremental testing practices [20]. However, TTS focuses predominantly on software testing and lacks alignment with the broader requirements of cyber-physical systems engineering. Furthermore, with SysML 2.0 moving away from UML foundations, the applicability of these approaches to modern MBSE practices becomes increasingly limited.

These limitations highlight the need for a systematic and scalable methodology tailored specifically for SysML-based environments, addressing traceability, integration, and alignment across the SE V-Model. This research aims to fill this gap by proposing a systematic MBTD framework leveraging SysML to bridge requirements and testing, integrating test case elements, requirement traceability, and black-box testing techniques to enhance the quality, consistency, and scalability of testing in SE projects.

4 Solution

4.1 SysML Status Quo

The SysML is a general-purpose modeling language specifically designed for systems engineering applications [21, 22]. Developed by the OMG, SysML extends UML to meet the needs of modeling complex systems, encompassing requirements, structure, behavior, and parametric analysis [21]. It serves as a foundational tool for MBSE, enabling the creation of comprehensive and traceable system models across various lifecycle stages [22].

While SysML supports robust system modeling capabilities, it lacks dedicated features for modeling detailed test design. Elements such as pre- and post-conditions, test steps, and test data play a critical role in creating structured and executable test cases but are not natively supported within SysML's current framework. Specifically, SysML 1.5 allows abstract test cases to be modeled within a SysML Requirement Diagram, where test cases can be traced back to their sources (requirements) using the <<verify>> relationship (see Fig. 1, modeled using Sparx Enterprise Architect (EA)[3]).

Two essential outcomes can be extracted from this feature within the SysML Requirement Diagram:

[3] https://sparxsystems.com/

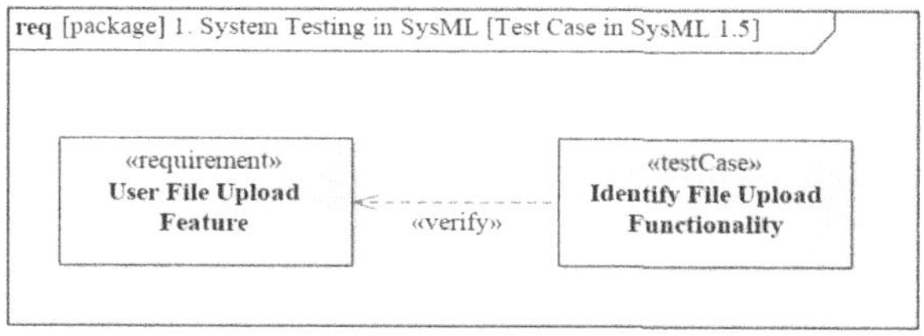

Fig. 1. Test Case Modeling in SysML 1.5 Version

1. System testing is a significant concern for MBSE as well as systems engineers.
2. Even though the feature is very abstract, the traceability between system requirements and test cases in SysML is vital.

However, a test case—or more broadly, a test design process—is not just about ensuring the connection between requirements and test cases. Test cases contain critical details necessary for verifying and validating system requirements. Therefore, the modeling possibilities in SysML are insufficient to fully capture the scope of a test case or to support effective system V&V.

Defining Test Case Elements with Meta Model

In the proposed strategy, the following test case elements have been selected based on their importance and relevance in providing a thorough and systematic approach to both test design and test execution:

- **Test Case ID:** A unique identifier for each test case, ensuring they are distinct, referenceable, and traceable.
- **Test Case Name:** A concise and descriptive title that summarizes the key purpose of the test case.
- **Test Objective:** A clear statement outlining the specific goals of the test, providing a rationale for its inclusion in the test suite.
- **Pre- and Post-conditions:** These specify the conditions that must be met before and after test case execution. Preconditions are essential for ensuring that the system is in the correct state before test initiation, while postconditions make sure that any adjustments made during testing are brought back to their default state, preparing the system for subsequent testing or test completion.
- **Test Steps:** A detailed sequence of actions performed during testing, starting with "Test Start" and finishing with "Test End".
- **Test Data:** The data inputs required for each test step execution.
- **Expected Results:** The anticipated outcomes based on the system's behavior and test data.

The clear identification of test cases via IDs, names, and objectives supports traceability throughout the system lifecycle. Moreover, pre- and post-conditions create a structured testing environment, while detailed steps, data, and expected results enable reliable and purposeful execution and evaluation.

In Fig. 2, you can see an overview of our MBTD approach by a meta-model using a UML class diagram style. In yellow we modeled the connection to the existing SysML diagram types, which are later on used to realize our MBTD. This meta-model facilitates the comprehension of the different test case elements used, their interrelations, and connections to SysML, visually.

Structural and Behavioral Test Case Elements

Each test case element detailed above has different functionalities, with static and dynamic aspects. Currently, SysML 1.5 does not provide a dedicated diagram that incorporates both. Therefore, a single SysML diagram type is insufficient and inconvenient for modeling the mentioned test case elements.

To integrate the desired test case elements into SysML diagrams effectively, it is essential to categorize each component based on whether it conveys a structural or behavioral aspect:

- **Structural Elements:** Test Case ID, Test Case Name, Test Objective, Preconditions, and Postconditions are structural elements, as they define the schema and conditions under which testing occurs. Structural diagrams in SysML, such as Block Definition Diagram (BDD), Internal Block Diagram (IBD), and Package Diagram, are well-suited for representing the static aspects of the system—its components, relationships, configurations, and organization [23]. The advantages of using structural diagrams for these test case elements include maintaining clear arrangements, hierarchical organization, traceability, and a concise definition of details.
- **Behavioral Elements:** Test Steps, Test Data, and Expected Results are classified as behavioral elements because they focus on dynamic system interactions and procedures during execution. Behavioral diagrams in SysML, such as Activity Diagrams, Sequence Diagrams, State Machine Diagrams, and Use Case Diagrams, are ideal for capturing these dynamic aspects, including processes, interactions, and workflows [23]. Using behavior diagrams allows for accurate and precise modeling of these test case elements in a process-centric manner while providing a clear visual representation of the test execution flow.

By defining structural test case elements through structural diagrams, the methodology ensures that important aspects such as test case aims, purposes, and conditions are fully understood. Meanwhile, behavioral test case elements are represented through behavioral diagrams, ensuring that the models accurately reflect the execution flow while avoiding oversight through clear visual representation. In short, distinguishing between static and dynamic test case elements allows for more precise modeling within SysML, leading to better traceability and alignment between system models and testing processes.

4.2 Modeling Test Cases with Our MBTD Approach

In this subsection, the MBTD framework, modeled to be used in real-case scenarios, will be introduced alongside abstract model examples. This will explain the methodological approach, modifications made to the selected SysML diagrams to suit test design functionalities, and ensure the strategy's reproducibility.

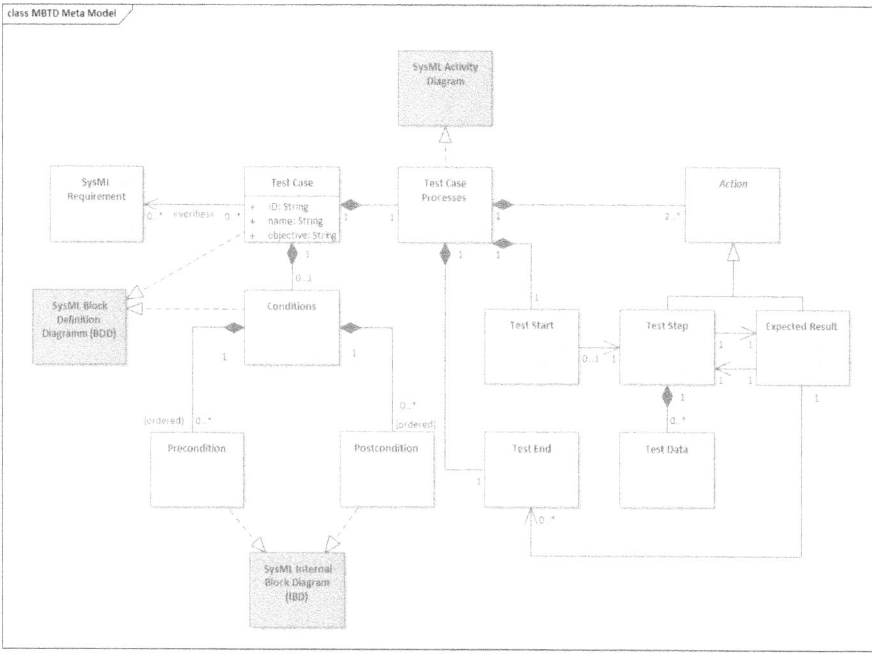

Fig. 2. MBTD UML Meta Model (connection to SysML diagram types are shown in yellow)

In addition to covering all the aforementioned test case elements according to their diagram types (structural and behavioral), this subsection will detail how requirement traceability was managed between the test case elements and system requirements through abstract model examples.

To achieve this, the subsection is categorized into three main parts: a test case overview that outlines the modeling approach for test case ID, name, objective, preconditions, and postconditions; test case processes that illustrate the strategy for modeling the test steps, test data, and expected results; and finally, the methodology established for securing traceability between test cases and system requirements, demonstrated through different modeling strategies.

To create the test case overview, test case processes, and requirement traceability, an example test case based on verifying a system's file upload and display functionalities will be used to reinforce understanding of the methodology applied in deploying the MBTD framework.

Test Case Overview Modeling

The modeling of the static test case elements employed BDD and IBD within SysML. The BDD was used to model the test case ID, name, and objective, and to provide a broad overview of the pre- and post-conditions (see Fig. 3).

Two primary blocks were established in the BDD for modeling the Test Case Overview. The first block is the <<Test Case>> block, which provides the test case identification and houses the Test Case ID, Test Case Name, and Test Objective. The

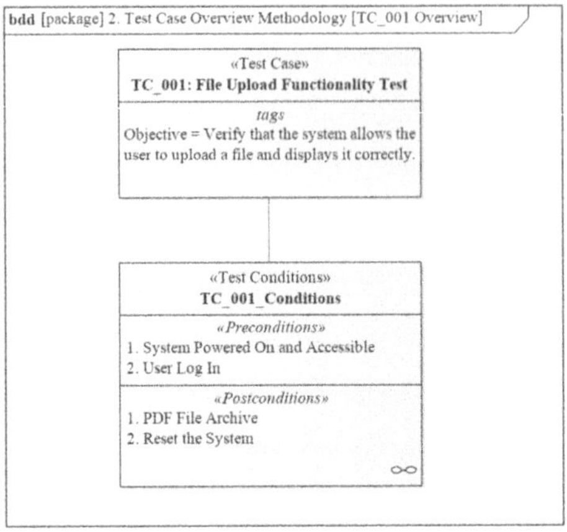

Fig. 3. SysML BDD for Test Case Overview Modeling

second block is the <<Test Conditions>> block, designated for articulating the pre- and post-conditions concisely.

For modeling the <<Test Case>> block, the default <<Block>> stereotype was modified to hold a custom stereotype. This was done to distinguish it from other blocks representing system components or other test design categories, serving as a starting point for the reviewer before exploring further test case elements. This also differentiates it from the existing <<testCase>> element (see Fig. 1), which is only available for use within the SysML Requirement Diagram. Thus, it was necessary to define a distinct stereotype to effectively encompass the identification elements of the test case and serve as an initiation point for any test case definition within MBTD in SysML.

The naming of the <<Test Case>> block is intended to hold both the Test Case ID and Test Case Name. This approach was chosen to facilitate easy reference and ensure that each test case is distinctly identified.

Although the Test Objective can be defined in various ways, such as directly as a block note, this may provide limitations for future usage. Considering the vital role of the <<Test Case>> block and the central importance of the test objective in articulating the necessity and goal of the test case, the "tags" functionality was found more suitable. As a result, the Test Objective was defined as a tagged value, labeled "Objective."

Tagged values offer several benefits, including adding customizable metadata (i.e., tagged values) in a structured and flexible manner, which supports the definition of additional elements relevant to test case descriptions. Tagged values are also searchable and can be used to generate reports or filter elements within SysML-compatible tools, making them a practical choice for capturing such information.

The same stereotyping logic was applied to the <<Test Conditions>> block as with the <<Test Case>> block. This differentiation not only clearly separates these blocks from other blocks within the overall system model but also clarifies their role and purpose within the MBTD framework. Furthermore, the <<Test Conditions>>

block serves as a modular container for the pre- and post-conditions, providing a brief overview before delving into specific details.

The block naming is anticipated to combine the Test Case ID with the block's functionality, resulting in "Test Case ID_Conditions." This ensures consistency in the MBTD framework structure and clearly indicates that the block's role is to contain the conditions of the test case under consideration.

To further understand how the pre- and post-conditions were defined and how the structure of the <<Test Conditions>> block was achieved, it is necessary to examine the applied modeling approach. Initially, two IBDs were created as child diagrams of the <<Test Conditions>> block to model each pre- and post-condition in detail. The method for modeling these conditions in SysML IBD will be demonstrated using the preconditions model (see Fig. 4), with the same approach applied to the postconditions.

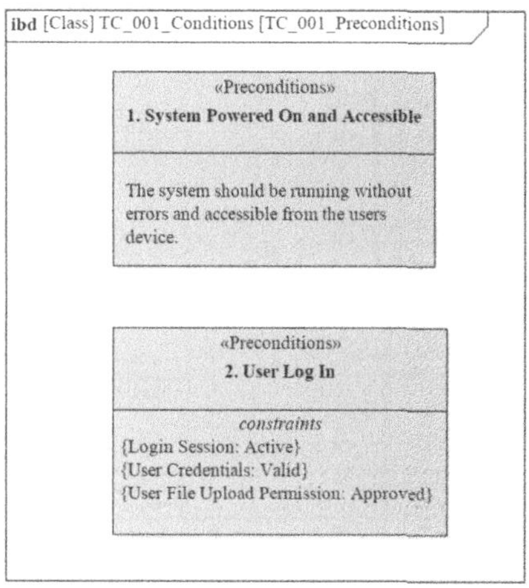

Fig. 4. Preconditions Modeling in SysML IBD

For each precondition, a property block is defined. The same logic, as in the previous cases, is used for stereotyping the property blocks with "<<Preconditions>>." A further advantage can be observed when checking the <<Test Conditions>> block (see Fig. 3), as stereotyping allows for the block to be divided into two categories, maintaining a clear structure.

The property blocks are named with numerical indexes followed by brief descriptions of the conditions. This approach maintains chronological order in the <<Test Conditions>> block while providing a summary of each condition. Since conditions represent the prerequisites that must be met before and after test execution for the test case to be valid, the details of each condition are defined using the "notes" and "constraints" properties within the property block. Notes clarify the specific requirements for each condition, while constraints specify the exact parameters that must be met, ensuring precision and reducing ambiguity.

Returning to the Test Case Overview BDD (Fig. 3), finally, the connection between the two blocks was established through an association relationship, underscoring their interdependence and indicating the essential nature of test conditions for the test case.

Test Case Processes Modeling

The SysML Activity Diagram is well-suited for modeling the dynamic elements of the test case design, as it effectively represents the sequence and flow of testing activities (see Fig. 5).

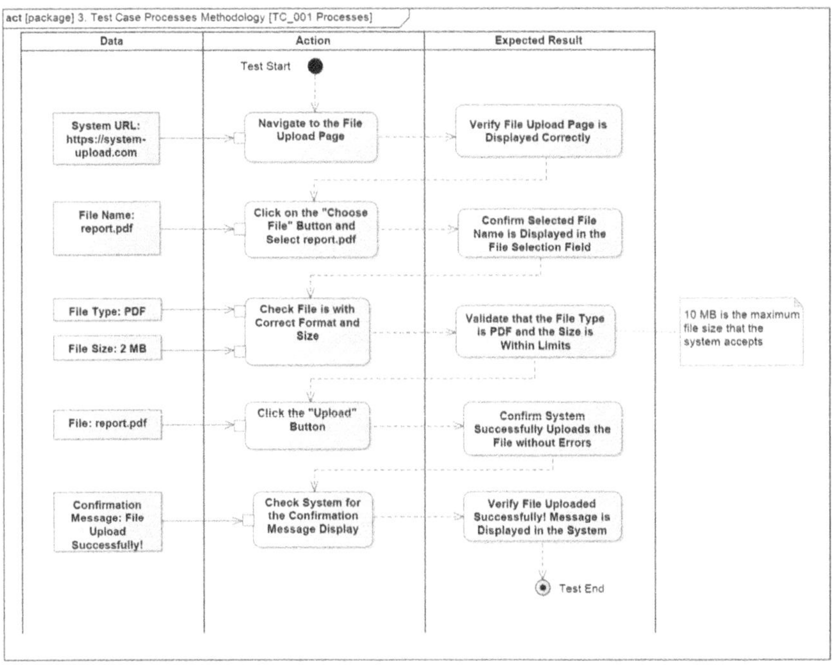

Fig. 5. SysML Activity Diagram for Test Case Processes Modeling

The first step in modeling the Test Steps, Test Data, and Expected Results was the creation and arrangement of three distinct partitions (swimlanes). The first partition, "Data," represents the Test Data required for each test step. The second partition, "Action," contains the Test Steps necessary to conduct the required testing activities. Finally, the "Expected Result" partition captures the desired system outcomes based on the requirements, test data, and steps. Each partition is placed vertically in the diagram for clarity and readability, following the sequence of processes required during test execution.

The "Test Start" initial node in the Action partition marks the beginning of test case execution, signaling the start of actions, with subsequent components defining the input data and expected system behaviors, leading to the final "Test End" node. Figure 5 further illustrates the detailed modeling approaches utilized within the activity diagram.

For instance, data utilized or generated during testing is categorized in the Data partition using Object Nodes, which serve as inputs for the corresponding test steps. These Object Nodes connect to the elements in the Action partition through Object Flow relationships, ensuring consistency with standard toolbox usage and reinforcing the representation of test data throughout the MBTD framework.

The Action partition employs Action elements to define test steps based on the input data and corresponding system behaviors. Action Pins on the left side of Action elements indicate data inputs, clarifying interactions between data points and test actions. A key benefit of Action Pins is their ability to represent multiple functionalities during the course of action. For example, two Action Pins on an Action element indicate that two separate system functions must be addressed during test step execution.

Similarly, the Expected Result partition uses Action elements to represent anticipated outcomes. In traditional test cases, expected results are defined based on the intended system behavior. Here, the goal is to define them as actions required by the tester to confirm the system's response to the previous test step. This ensures that the tester remains engaged throughout the verification process and confirms that the system performs as expected.

Connections from the Action partition to the Expected Result partition, and to subsequent test steps in the Action partition, are established using Control Flows. These illustrate the sequence of operations that must be followed and executed by the tester.

Since both Object Flow and Control Flow relationships have the same default appearance, Control Flows were modified to appear as dashed lines. This distinction helps maintain clarity by separating the data required for testing from the controlled actions that need to be performed by the tester during the test.

To keep the definitions within the partition elements short and precise, notes were used to provide additional information or clarifications as needed, maintaining consistency in Test Case Processes modeling. An advantage of implementing notes is the flexibility they offer. For instance, besides detailing individual elements, they can be used to provide general notes applicable to the overall test execution process.

Each element within the toolbox was carefully selected and utilized to convey accurate and relevant information about the testing procedures, adhering to the intended functionalities of the SysML activity diagram.

Requirement Traceability Modeling

While the methodology outlines how to design comprehensive test cases using SysML diagrams, one critical aspect remains: the traceability between test cases and system requirements.

The SysML Requirement diagram (see Fig. 1) offers traceability using the <<testCase>> element and <<verify>> relationship link. However, when test cases are modeled through the outlined methodology, the <<testCase>> element becomes ineffective. To strengthen the MBTD framework and ensure robust traceability, a more structured and flexible approach was required.

This strategy utilizes the SysML Requirement Diagram. By leveraging the diagram's inherent capabilities and extending them, a more flexible and detailed methodology is implemented.

To address the essential role of traceability, two distinct models were developed within the SysML Requirement diagram: a High-Level Requirement Traceability model and a Detailed Requirement Traceability model. These models offer adaptable solutions for improving traceability representation.

High-Level Requirement Traceability Modeling

The first approach to modeling traceability is the high-level view (see Fig. 6). This view models the abstract traceability between system requirements and the derived test case. The goal is to show which requirements the test case aims to verify, focusing on a high-level perspective without delving into details.

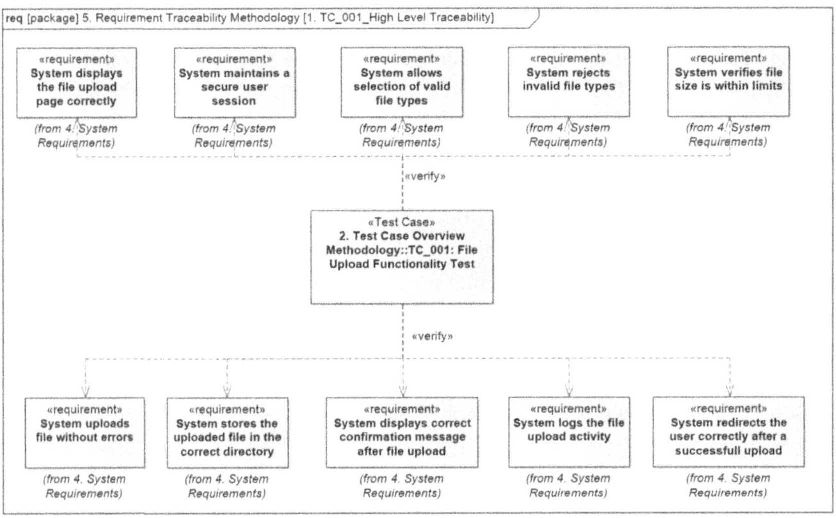

Fig. 6. High-Level Requirement Traceability in SysML Requirement Diagram

To model this, the <<Test Case>> block, which contains the test case ID, name, and objective, along with the relevant requirements, are placed into the diagram. The <<Test Case>> block is centrally positioned, while the corresponding requirements are placed around it. Details such as the test objective, requirement ID, and requirement text are omitted to avoid clutter and maintain focus on traceability. However, this is a strategic choice and can be customized as needed.

The <<Test Case>> block is linked to each requirement via a <<verify>> relationship, emphasizing the test case's role in confirming the implementation of each requirement. It's important to note that the <<verify>> relationship can be customized to reflect the nature of the linkage, and annotations, such as notes, can also be added to enhance traceability.

The focus here is to maintain a clean and streamlined representation, providing a clear view of which requirements are being verified by the test case and allowing for a quick understanding of the test coverage.

Detailed Requirement Traceability Modeling

Traditionally, detailed traceability, often managed through a Requirements Traceability Matrix (RTM), links each test step to its corresponding system requirements. However, relying on separate documentation, such as Word or Excel, for this traceability proves inefficient and disconnected from the MBTD framework.

To address this, a Detailed Requirement Traceability model (see Fig. 7) within the SysML framework was necessary for a cohesive MBTD approach, integrating the RTM's functionality directly within the model. This integration ensures that each test step's verification of system requirements is explicitly mapped, enhancing traceability.

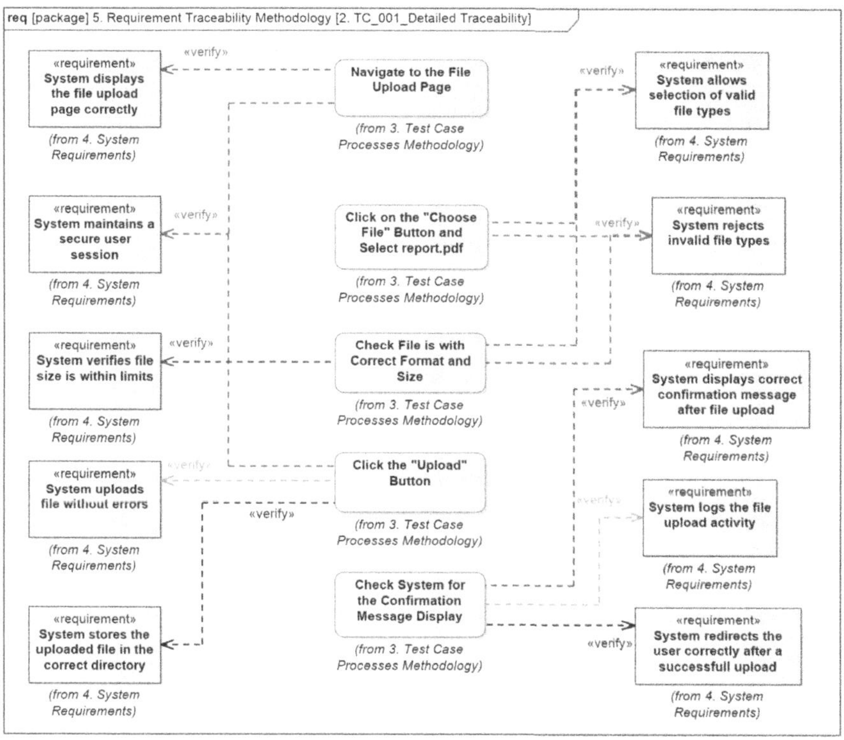

Fig. 7. Detailed Requirement Traceability Modeling in SysML Requirement Diagram

For modeling, the test steps from the outlined Test Case Processes were placed into the diagram, maintaining their original sequential order. In a similar manner to High-Level Requirement Traceability, the relevant requirements were incorporated and logically distributed around the test steps.

Since a test step may verify more than one requirement, connections between test steps and system requirements were modeled with special attention. To maintain clarity, different color codes were assigned to the <<verify>> relationships. While creating the Detailed Requirement Traceability model involves simple drag-and-drop actions, several adjustments were made to ensure clarity and readability. This approach is suitable for test cases with fewer steps or requirements but may not be ideal for more complex scenarios.

Despite these limitations, this model is advantageous for everyone involved in the project: systems engineers can ensure alignment and coverage, testers can better grasp the testing scope, and technical teams can address issues more effectively. As a result, alternative solutions were explored to make Detailed Requirement Traceability modeling feasible for more complex cases, while addressing potential challenges.

Relation Matrix View

The breakthrough came with the use of the "Switch to Relation Matrix View" feature, accessible by right-clicking on the diagram tab or through the EA Browser tool. This feature transforms the traditional requirement diagram view into a relation matrix, emulating an RTM.

When applied to the Detailed Requirement Traceability model, the matrix view (see Fig. 8) effectively visualizes the relationships between test steps and system requirements, fulfilling the goals of an RTM without needing additional tools. The matrix settings are adjusted to designate action elements (test steps) as sources and requirements as targets.

Target / Source	System all...	System dis...	System dis...	System log...	System ma...	System red...	System rej...	System sto...	System up...	System veri...
Check File ...	Verify						Verify			Verify
Check Sy...		Verify		Verify		Verify				
Click on th...	Verify						Verify			
Click the "...					Verify			Verify	Verify	
Navigate to...			Verify		Verify					

Fig. 8. Detailed Requirement Traceability as a Table Matrix

Each cell in the matrix corresponds to a specific test step verifying a system requirement, while empty cells indicate no verification for that requirement.

This matrix feature drastically reduces the need for meticulous organization of test steps, requirements, and verification links within the Detailed Requirement Traceability model. The primary focus shifts to ensuring accurate connections between test steps and corresponding requirements. As a result, the need for extensive focus on readability and clarity diminishes, as the Relation Matrix View presents the Detailed Requirement Traceability clearly and comprehensively.

In summary, these strategies ensure that the traceability aspect of MBTD is not only methodologically sound but also adaptable to various levels of detail and complexity.

4.3 Black-Box Testing Techniques (What is Included in Our Approach and Why?)

Before moving on to the validation of the methodology, it is essential to emphasize the comprehensiveness of the MBTD framework, particularly through the inclusion of black-box testing techniques. This inclusion unifies the framework by addressing every aspect necessary for an effective and efficient test design process through modeling approaches.

While SysML supports the use of Use Case and State Machine diagrams, facilitating the modeling of use case and state transition testing techniques, other black-box testing techniques, such as Equivalence Partitioning (EP), Boundary Value Analysis (BVA), Decision Table Testing, and Pair-Wise Testing, require tabular representations. Although SysML lacks a dedicated diagram type for tables, it allows the creation of custom tables within its diagrams, enabling the integration of these tabular-based black-box testing techniques (see Fig. 9) directly into the SysML framework.

TC_001: Equivalence Partition Table

Parameter	Equivalence Partition	Input Data	Expected Output
File Type	PDF, DOCX, JPEG	PDF	File is accepted for upload
File Size	0 < File Size ≤ 10 MB	2 MB	Fiel is accepted for upload

Fig. 9. Equivalence Partition Black-Box Testing Technique in SysML Activity Diagram

In the proposed strategy, the tabular black-box testing techniques are integrated with the test case processes in the activity diagram, serving both to define processes and support test execution. This approach ensures that test data is easy to reference and enhances understanding and efficiency in both the test design and execution phases.

With this final addition, the research supports a fully integrated test design framework where all aspects of system-level testing can be managed within SysML.

5 Validation of the Approach

5.1 Sample Project: Digital Twin of a High-Voltage Cable

To validate our proposed solution, we applied it in an engineering project at the South Westphalia University of Applied Sciences. This project is about building a Digital Twin of a high-voltage earth cable system to monitor cables in real time and analyze and optimize their usage over their lifetime [24]. We refer to it as the Digital Twin Cable System (DTCS).

The system is divided into three main components (see Fig. 10): the sensor box with an energy harvesting system (Micro Controller Station, MCS), the frontend (MQTT Broker, Node-RED), and the backend (MongoDB Database, Power Performance Monitoring (PPM) Dashboard, see also Fig. 11).

The sensor box with an energy harvesting system contains sensors to measure data from the Cable System, such as voltage, temperature, and current. It is designed to provide

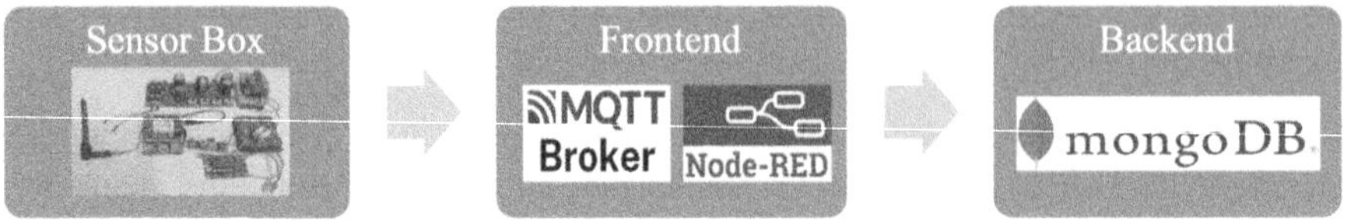

Fig. 10. The main components of the DTCS[4,5,6]

a self-sustaining power supply to the DTCS hardware components and incorporates a battery management system to optimize battery charge cycles and overall health. The sensor box harvests energy from the magnetic field of the Cable System and includes various safety mechanisms to ensure reliability and safety.

Moreover, the sensor box transmits the collected data via mobile communication to the Node-RED frontend, using MQTT as the communication standard. This frontend is located in a cloud system. From here the data is transferred to an on-premise data center into a MongoDB for data storage. The PPM Dashboard is then used to display the data for a selected cable. In the example shown in Fig. 11, the voltage over time is displayed for a specific measuring point on a selected cable over a chosen time period.

In summary, our example project demonstrates the characteristics of a cyber-physical system. It combines the domains of hardware, electrical, electronic, and software. This fulfills the need for an SE approach to model the whole system, before going into the different domains and in the end to provide a system test of the implemented solution. The test approach uses SysML models from the early phase of development as a test basis. In the following subsection, we discuss how our approach from Sect. 4 was applied to the DTCS.

5.2 Application of Our MBTD Approach

In the project, 156 requirements were modeled. Based on these, a system context diagram and a system component diagram were derived (both based on a SysML BDD). To establish a solid basis for system testing, we also modeled different system processes using activity flow diagrams (SysML Activity Diagram).

In the final step, test cases were modeled to align with selected system requirements, capturing all relevant aspects of the test design process. Both positive and negative test cases were modeled to ensure a comprehensive approach. All aspects of the system and the proposed MBTD framework were modeled using Sparx EA, as defined in Sect. 4. Furthermore, the tooling allowed us to automatically view test case requirements coverage and supported the modeling of traces between requirements and test cases.

While the test designer's feedback was positive, particularly highlighting the benefits of integrating test cases and requirements within a single model, certain challenges remained. Specifically, the manual effort required for modeling test cases and establishing traceability was noted as a limitation. Additionally, the validation process

[4] https://www.mongodb.com/

[5] https://nodered.org/

[6] https://mqtt.org/

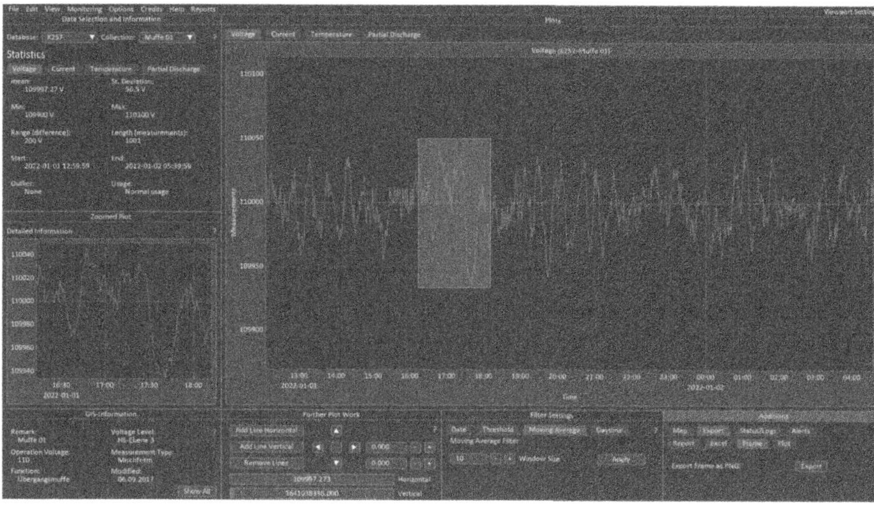

Fig. 11. Power Performance Monitoring Dashboard

was qualitative, focusing on a subset of high-priority requirements rather than all 156 requirements, with the prioritization based on their criticality within the project scope.

This validation serves as a proof of concept for the proposed MBTD framework, demonstrating its applicability in a real-world system development context.

In the next section, we discuss the results of our validation, along with potential further steps that could be investigated.

6 Discussion of Results and Outlook

6.1 Discussion of Results

To discuss the results of our contribution, we revisit the research questions from Sect. 2.

RQ1.1: If MBSE today does not include Test Design, how can we interrelate both?

Our approach presents a novel way to not only interrelate but also integrate MBSE and MBTD within a single modeling environment. By reusing existing diagram types for test design, our methodology enables today's SE tools (like EA) to adopt and directly start applying the framework. Through a qualitative validation approach, we demonstrated the feasibility of this integration in the environment of cyber-physical systems, focusing on a subset of high-priority requirements.

RQ1.2: How can we measure and improve the Quality of Testing based on this interrelation?

Our approach provides a well-defined traceability structure that facilitates quality checks and, ultimately, improvement. It enables the identification of uncovered requirements and test cases lacking requirement traceability, both of which indicate potential quality issues in the testing process. Furthermore, the integration of system requirements and test design within a single modeling environment fosters collaboration between systems engineers and test designers. However, manual effort is still required for modeling traces, which poses challenges as the complexity of the system and its models increases, potentially leading to difficulties in maintaining an overview and avoiding mistakes.

The overarching question, "**RQ1:** How can we ensure good quality of Testing in MBSE?" is addressed by our approach in the following way:

Our proposed methodology offers benefits beyond the technical aspects of system V&V. It enhances communication and collaboration among all stakeholders, including systems engineers, developers, testers, end-users, and company owners. This integrated approach promotes a shared understanding of system goals and requirements, reduces the risk of miscommunication, and leads to a more streamlined and efficient development process. Additionally, the focus on traceability, consistency, and alignment with ongoing changes in rapid, complex system developments ensures that the final product meets the needs and expectations of all stakeholders, providing confidence in the system's quality and reliability.

6.2 Outlook

The MBTD approach could be further enhanced by adding traces to other diagrams, such as component and activity flow diagrams. Thereby the test coverage could be more precisely measured to find testing gaps. Additionally, Artificial Intelligence (AI) methods could be used to semi-automate or validate manually created traces between test cases and other SE diagram elements, reducing redundancy and streamlining the modeling process.

Another potential enhancement involves exploring other existing SysML diagrams to automate the test design process. For instance, test steps could be derived automatically from SysML activity diagrams based on defined coverage criteria. This would enable better reuse of models while significantly decreasing the manual modeling effort.

Furthermore, OMG and INCOSE recently released SysML version 2.0 [25], which introduces fundamental changes to the language. Our approach requires adaptation to this new version. In SysML 2.0 a so-called "verification case", which is still similar to the SysML 1.5 "test case", is available. Yet still lacks the modeling expressiveness that our approach addresses. Additionally, further evaluation of existing methodologies such as the UTP and the TTS approach could inform improvements to our framework. However, it is important to note that SysML 2.0 is no longer based on UML, which could limit the applicability of UML-based methodologies.

Another extension could be the test execution aspect. Currently, our approach supports only test case design, requiring an additional tool while executing tests to gather results and versioning test runs. Integrating test execution capabilities into the MBTD framework could further streamline the testing process.

Last but not least, further modeling of concrete SE projects could help improve the approach by revealing missing modeling aspects or addressing complexity-related issues, contributing to the continued refinement and scalability of the methodology.

Acknowledgments. We like to thank the High Voltage Lab of Prof. Dr. Robert Bach and his team at the South Westphalia University of Applied Sciences. Their project on the Digital Twin of an underground high-voltage cable gave us the opportunity to validate our approach on a real-world example of a cyber-physical system.

References

1. INCOSE: Systems Engineering HANDBOOK V5, Wiley (2023)
2. Haberfellner, R., et al.: Systems Engineering, Birkhäuser (2019)
3. Systems Engineering Tools Home Page. https://www.systemsengineeringtool.com. Accessed 06 Sep 2024
4. INCOSE: SYSTEMS ENGINEERING vision 2035. http://www.incose.org (2021)
5. OMG: SysML, http://www.omgsysml.org. Accessed 06 Sep 2024
6. Wymore, A.: Model-Based Systems Engineering, CRC Press (2018)
7. Weilkiens, T.: Systems Engineering with SysML/UML, Elsevier (2008)
8. Jacklin, S. et al.: Verification, validation, and certification challenges for adaptive flight-critical control system software. In: AIAA Guidance, Navigation, and Control Conference and Exhibit, American Institute of Aeronautics and Astronautics (2004)
9. Sami, M.: The Validation and Verification Model – The V-Model. https://melsatar.blog/2018/08/27/the-validation-and-verification-model-the-v-model/. Accessed 24 Sep 2024
10. Spillner, A., Linz T.: Software Testing Foundations: A Study Guide for the Certified Tester Exam: Foundation Level, ISTQB Compliant, 5th, revised and updated edition, dpunkt.verlag (2021)
11. Wübbeke, A.: Variabilitätsmanagement in Anforderungs- und Testfallspezifikation für Software-Produktlinien, University of Paderborn (2010)
12. Huldt, T., Stenius, I.: State-of-practice survey of model-based systems engineering. Syst. Eng. **22**(2), 134–145 (2019)
13. Madni, A.M., Sievers, M.: Model-based systems engineering: motivation, current status, and research opportunities. Syst. Eng. **21**(3), 172–190 (2018)
14. Kjeldaas, K.A., Haugen, R.A., Syverud, E.: Challenges in detecting emergent behavior in system testing. INCOSE Int. Symp. **31**(1), 1211–1228 (2021)
15. Gomes De Oliveira Neto, F., Horkoff, J., Knauss, E., Kasauli, R., Liebel, G.: Challenges of aligning requirements engineering and system testing in large-scale agile: a multiple case study. In: 2017 IEEE 25th International Requirements Engineering Conference Workshops (REW), pp. 315–322. IEEE, Lisbon (2017)
16. Bringmann, E., Krämer, A.: Model-based testing of automotive systems. In: 1st International Conference on Software Testing, Verification, and Validation, pp. 485–493. IEEE, Lillehammer (2008)
17. Wang, G., Pavalkis, S.: A model-based V&V test strategy based on emerging system modeling techniques. INCOSE Int. Symp. **29**(1), 771–787 (2019)
18. Walker, J., Borky, J.M.: Test planning, documentation, and impact analysis with SysML. ITEA J. Test Eval. **41**(4), 258–266 (2020)
19. UML Testing Profile 2 (UTP 2) Specification, https://www.omg.org/spec/UTP2/2.2/PDF. Accessed 08 Jan 2025
20. Felderer, M., Zech, P., Breu, R.: An agile and tool-supported methodology for model-driven system testing of service-centric systems. In: Agile and Lean Service-Oriented Development: Foundations, Theory, and Practice, pp. 238–253. IGI Global, Hershey (2013)
21. WHAT IS SYSML? https://www.omgsysml.org/what-is-sysml.htm. Accessed 08 Jan 2025
22. SysML FAQ: What is the Systems Modeling Language (SysML)?. https://sysml.org/sysml-faq/what-is-sysml.html. Accessed 08 Jan 2025
23. Hause, M.: The SysML modeling language. In: Fifteenth European Systems Engineering Conference, vol. 9, pp. 1–12. INCOSE, Gloucestershire (2006)
24. Bach, R. et al.: Concept and development of a digital twin of a 110-kV-cable line. CIGRE Paris Session 2024, Paris (2024)
25. OMG: SysML 2.0. https://www.omg.org/spec/SysML/2.0/Beta2/About-SysML. Accessed 03 Oct 2024

Effective Black Box Testing of Sentiment Analysis Classification Networks

Parsa Karbasizadeh[1], Fathiyeh Faghih[2(✉)], and Pouria Golshanrad[1]

[1] College of Engineering, Department of Electrical and Computer Engineering, University of Tehran, Tehran, Iran
parsa.karbasi@ut.ac.ir, pouria.golshanrad@ut.ac.ir

[2] fortiss GmbH, Munich, Germany
faghih@fortiss.org

Abstract. Transformer-based neural networks have demonstrated remarkable performance in natural language processing tasks such as sentiment analysis. Nevertheless, the issue of ensuring the dependability of these complicated architectures through comprehensive testing is still open. This paper presents a collection of coverage criteria specifically designed to assess test suites created for transformer-based sentiment analysis networks. Our approach utilizes input space partitioning, a black-box method, by considering emotionally relevant linguistic features such as verbs, adjectives, adverbs, and nouns. To effectively produce test cases that encompass a wide range of emotional elements, we utilize the k-projection coverage metric. This metric minimizes the complexity of the problem by examining subsets of k features at the same time, hence reducing dimensionality. Large language models are employed to generate sentences that display specific combinations of emotional features. Experiments demonstrate that test generation guided by our criteria increases test coverage by 16%, while reducing accuracy by 6.5%, thus exposing vulnerabilities.

Keywords: AI Dependability · Test · Transformers · Coverage Criteria · Sentiment Analysis

1 Introduction

The impact of neural networks on various fields, including image recognition, natural language processing, and self-driving cars, has been significant. In the context of Natural Language Processing (NLP), neural networks have gained notable recognition due to their ability to enhance accuracy [5]. Sentiment analysis, also known as opinion mining or emotion AI, is a natural language processing (NLP) technique used to determine the emotional tone or subjective opinion expressed in text. This procedure utilizes NLP methodologies to analyze and interpret human language, enabling diverse applications across various domains. For instance, in marketing, sentiment analysis can be leveraged

J. Fischbach et al. (Eds.): SWQD 2025, LNBIP 544, pp. 36–48, 2025.
https://doi.org/10.1007/978-3-031-89277-6_3

to evaluate customer opinions about products and services, providing valuable insights for brand reputation management. Various tools, including NLTK [3], are employed to interpret customer sentiment and capture embedded emotions.

Traditional emotion recognition methods struggle with complexities like word ambiguity, sarcasm, and negation. For example, the emotional connotation of a word like "overwhelmed" can vary depending on context. Transformers address these challenges through attention mechanisms and large-scale pre-training, capturing long-range dependencies and subtle emotional nuances [19].

Ensuring the reliability of transformer-based models through comprehensive testing remains a challenge. Conventional methods like neuron coverage [14] are prohibitively expensive due to transformers' scale and complexity. To address this, we propose novel coverage criteria using input space partitioning, focusing on emotionally relevant linguistic features like verbs, adjectives, adverbs, and nouns. We employ the k-projection coverage method to systematically explore the input space, enabling efficient test case generation [6].

Our approach achieves a 16% increase in test coverage, meaning the generated test cases cover a wider range of emotional scenarios and feature combinations in the input space. This enhanced coverage led to a 6.5% decrease in the accuracy of the System-Under-Test (SUT), demonstrating the effectiveness of our approach in uncovering additional faults. Our contributions include:

- Novel coverage criteria for black-box testing of sentiment analysis systems.
- A methodology for generating targeted test cases using large language models (LLMs).
- Validation of the criteria through improved fault detection.

Related Work: This paper explores concepts related to test generation, black-box testing, and model coverage in DNN models. It summarizes the current state of coverage and performance measures for DNN models and discusses previous research on utilizing diversity in black-box DNN testing to evaluate DNNs and conventional software systems [12,14].

Transformers are preferred over traditional DNNs due to their superior accuracy, particularly in AI domains like sentiment analysis [17]. Evaluating the adequacy of test suites for emotional sentiment analysis networks poses a significant challenge. In software engineering, test suite effectiveness is assessed through black-box and white-box testing [9]. Applying white-box criteria to transformer-based NLP systems is limited by their complexity and internal access requirements. Alternative testing methods such as black-box strategies or input diversity metrics may be necessary to ensure their reliability [1].

Input space partitioning is an effective approach for black-box testing, particularly in text data, where emotionally relevant features can be used to partition the input domain into smaller subsets for precise test case design [15].

k-projection coverage, employing dimensionality reduction, shows promise in image recognition for evaluating self-driving car perception systems using CNN-based neural networks and GAN-based models [6]. However, its potential in text-based emotional sentiment analysis remains unexplored.

The contributions of our study are as follows:

1. We introduce novel coverage criteria based on k-projection for black-box testing of sentiment analysis systems. This metric serves a dual purpose: evaluating the effectiveness of existing test suites and guiding the generation of new test cases to augment them.
2. Our experimental results demonstrate that enriching test suites using this proposed coverage criterion leads to a significant reduction in model accuracy. This finding has two key implications:
   - The coverage criterion is a valid metric for assessing test suites in this context, as higher coverage scores correlate with a greater ability to uncover faults and decrease model accuracy.
   - The coverage criterion can be effectively utilized to generate effective test cases that reveal failures and thus improve the overall quality of test suites.

The remainder of this paper is organized as follows. We explain the proposed methodology in Sect. 2, followed by a presentation of the experimental results in Sect. 3. Section 4 concludes the paper by summarizing our findings and future work.

2 Methodology

The performance of a neural network is typically evaluated by calculating its accuracy on a test suite. However, accuracy alone is not a sufficient measure of model quality. The effectiveness of testing and the reliability of the results heavily depend on the adequacy of the test suite. Coverage criteria are metrics used to assess how effectively a test suite exercises different aspects of a system under test. In traditional software testing, common criteria include statement, branch, and path coverage [8]. However, these traditional criteria cannot be directly applied to learning models due to their fundamentally different architecture [1]. To overcome this challenge, we propose a set of black-box metrics for evaluating test suites specifically designed for sentiment analysis tasks.

Our approach originates from Input Space Partitioning (ISP), a black-box software testing technique. ISP involves dividing a system's input domain into distinct subsets or partitions, where each partition represents inputs expected to result in similar system behavior. Test cases are then strategically selected from each partition to ensure comprehensive coverage of the input space.

2.1 Input Space Partitioning

The primary objective of this study is to assess the effectiveness of utilizing the input space partitioning technique to evaluate test suites for emotional sentiment analysis in Transformer-based neural networks. This technique utilizes the features of the input data to partition the input space into distinct regions, facilitating organization and understanding of the data. [6]

The architecture of the neural network model and the nature of the input data require the identification and selection of appropriate features for input space partitioning. Effective evaluation of a test suite requires developing a feature space that covers a wide range of scenarios and real-world instances. An effective feature space can be established by adherence to the guidelines proposed in Cheng et al.'s study [6], which outlines specific autonomous driving scenarios that the test cases should encompass and which will be defined subsequently.

To establish a clear foundation for the framework discussed in this study, we introduce the following notations. These notations are essential to understanding the subsequent mathematical definitions and analyses.

1. **Input Domain**: The input domain includes all textual inputs the neural network can receive. All text variations the network must process and respond to are included.
$$D = \{d_1, d_2, \ldots\}$$
where d_i represents an individual input text.
2. **Partition**: To understand the existing components and assess the test suite, it is crucial to establish specific partitions and map the input domain within those defined partitions. In this study, partitions are defined as follows:
$$P = \{P_1, P_2, \ldots, P_k\}$$
where $P_i \subseteq D$ and $P_i \cap P_j = \emptyset$ for $i \neq j$, and $\bigcup_{i=1}^{k} P_i = D$. Each partition P_j groups inputs that share specific combinations of emotional features (e.g., verbs, adjectives, adverbs, and nouns), as defined in Sect. 2.2. However, inputs within the same partition may produce different sentiment labels depending on the overall context of the sentence.
3. **Features**: Through the analysis of the input domain and the consideration of the functionality of the system under test (SUT), we can determine the important features that will be used to establish partitions.
$$F = \{F_1, F_2, \ldots, F_m\}$$
4. **Test Suite**: Representative tests should be selected from each partition to form a test suite.
$$T = \{t_1, t_2, \ldots, t_l\}$$
where $t_i \in P_j$ for some $P_j \in P$.

2.2 Emotional Features

Input space partitioning relies on specific features to establish partitions, crucial for evaluating test suite effectiveness in neural networks. The upcoming section will outline the specific features employed in this study.

The meaning and sentiment of a sentence can be identified through crucial components such as verbs, adverbs, adjectives, and other linguistic elements. Therefore, features are determined according to these important elements of a sentence. Verbs strongly influence a sentence's sentiment. For instance, in "She laughed when I saw her," the verb "laughed" implies joy, highlighting its importance in sentiment analysis. Besides the verb, the adverb in a sentence is another influential feature affecting its sentiment. For example, in "He bites his nails nervously," the adverb "nervously" alone can convey fear or anxiety, making its presence significant for sentence categorization.

Adjectives shape a sentence's emotional tone by describing specific feelings. For example, "She received a joyful gift" conveys happiness, whereas "She received a disappointing gift" indicates sadness. Nouns contribute significantly to a sentence's emotion. In "The old man sat alone, his eyes filled with tears, mourning the loss of his dearest friend," nouns like "tears" and "loss" contribute to its "sad" emotional label. The five emotional labels-joy, anger, sadness, fear, and surprise-were chosen as the primary labels for this study because they represent the most common and distinct emotional categories in sentiment analysis. These labels align with Ekman's basic emotions theory [7], which identifies these emotions as universal across cultures and supported by cross-cultural studies on facial expressions and physiological responses. In this research, the emotional attributes of nouns were integrated as an additional feature alongside verbs, adjectives, and adverbs. The sets of features presented in this paper are denoted as:

$$F = \{S_V, S_{ADJ}, S_{ADV}, S_N\}$$

where:

- S_V represents sentiment scores for verbs, categorized into emotional labels:

$$S_V : V \rightarrow \{\text{joy}, \text{anger}, \text{sadness}, \text{fear}, \text{surprise}\}$$

- S_{ADJ} represents sentiment scores for adjectives, categorized into emotional labels:

$$S_{ADJ} : ADJ \rightarrow \{\text{joy}, \text{anger}, \text{sadness}, \text{fear}, \text{surprise}\}$$

- S_{ADV} represents sentiment scores for adverbs, categorized into emotional labels:

$$S_{ADV} : ADV \rightarrow \{\text{joy}, \text{anger}, \text{sadness}, \text{fear}, \text{surprise}\}$$

- S_N represents sentiment scores for nouns, categorized into emotional labels, including a neutral category:

$$S_N : N \rightarrow \{\text{joy}, \text{anger}, \text{sadness}, \text{fear}, \text{surprise}, \text{neutral}\}$$

When dealing with multiple features and their numerous potential values, the number of possible combinations can grow exponentially. This can make generating comprehensive input data, encompassing all features at once, extremely complex. k-projection coverage is a technique used in input space partitioning to overcome this challenge. It aims to systematically explore the input space by focusing on a subset of 'k' parameters at a time, while keeping the remaining parameters fixed.

To illustrate this method, consider an example of four features $\{F_1, F_2, F_3, F_4\}$, each taking two values $\{0, 1\}$, resulting in a total of $2^4 = 16$ possible combinations. Applying k-projection coverage with different values of k results in the following:

- $k = 1$ (Single Feature Projection): We focus on one feature at a time, keeping the others fixed.
  - Number of projections: 4 (one for each feature)
  - Number of cases per projection: 2 (the two possible values of the feature)
- $k = 2$ (Pairwise Projection): We focus on pairs of features, keeping the other two fixed.
  - Number of projections: 6 (combinations of 4 features taken 2 at a time)
  - Number of cases per projection: 4 (2 values for each of the two features)
- $k = 3$ (Three-way Projection): We focus on groups of three features, keeping the remaining one fixed.
  - Number of projections: 4 (combinations of 4 features taken 3 at a time)
  - Number of cases per projection: 8 (2 values for each of the three features)
- $k = 4$ (All Features Projection): We consider all features simultaneously.
  - Number of projections: 1
  - Number of cases per projection: 16 (all possible combinations)

Expanding on the previous example, this approach systematically selects sets of k features and strives to achieve comprehensive coverage within a newly formed reduced dimension. This technique of dimensionality reduction enables efficient test generation, as it requires fewer test cases to achieve complete coverage of the input space.

Generally, to calculate the coverage rate for k = n, where n is the number of problem features, the following formula is employed:

$$\text{COV} = \frac{C(D)}{\alpha^n} \tag{1}$$

In the above equation, $C(D)$ represents the coverage rate of the test data over possible states, where α is the range of each feature and n is the problem's dimensionality. In our context, $\alpha = 6$ and $n = 4$, requiring 1296 unique test data points for full coverage. This approach, however, is computationally demanding and requires substantial test data.

Alternatively, when considering the effect of k, the following formula is used:

$$\text{COV} = \frac{C(D)}{\binom{n}{k}\alpha^k} \tag{2}$$

Considering the inverse correlation of the denominator, it is evident that the denominator, which is affected by variables such as k, α, and n, greatly decreases the number of tests needed to achieve complete coverage.

Incorporating all four features in sentences can be challenging and costly, reducing sentence clarity. Thus, this approach is ineffective. To tackle this issue, the dimensions of the feature coverage space are reduced, with the variable k

being set to values of 2 and 3 in this study. The values for the variable k are compared in Sect. 3 to evaluate their individual effects.

After measuring the coverage achieved by the test suite to assess the effectiveness of the k-projection metric, we attempt to increase coverage by generating test cases for uncovered scenarios. Ultimately, we explore whether improving coverage aids in the detection of hidden flaws in existing sentiment analysis networks.

2.3 Evaluation of the Coverage Criteria

Our approach to evaluating the proposed coverage criterion involves examining whether increasing a test suite's coverage score uncovers more failures in the sentiment analysis model. We introduce a method for augmenting test suites with additional test cases specifically designed to improve their coverage score. This evaluation method has two key advantages:

- **Validation of Coverage Criteria**: Observing a decrease in model accuracy when using the augmented test suite confirms the effectiveness of the coverage criteria for evaluating sentiment analysis test suites. A higher coverage score indicates a greater ability to identify faults and lower model accuracy, thus validating the criteria.
- **Practical Test Case Generation**: The proposed method offers practitioners a valuable tool for generating effective test cases in sentiment analysis tasks. By focusing on increasing coverage, practitioners can systematically identify and address potential weaknesses in their models.

To uncover unexplored regions within the test suite based on our proposed coverage criteria, we propose a strategy for generating novel sentences. Manual sentence creation, while a viable method for producing desired test cases, is both time-intensive and unsuitable for generating large quantities.

Our idea in this study is to use Large Language Models (LLMs) [11] to generate the required sentences. LLMs require training using huge quantities of textual data, which allows them to imitate human-like text production. Examples of such LLMs include GPT-3 [4] and LaMDA [18]. In this study, we employed Claude 3 Opus [2], an LLM produced by Anthropic, which is recognized for its exceptional sentence generation capabilities.

When utilizing LLMs for test generation, explicit prompts play a crucial role in guiding the model to produce specific types of test data that align with the research objectives. By evaluating the datasets using defined features in Sect. 2, it is apparent that this dataset does not contain inputs with mixed emotions. For instance, after analyzing the test suites, we identified that the test suite lacks sentences where a verb is labeled with *sadness* and an adverb is labeled with *joy*. We generate such a test case using the following formulaic approach:

Let S represent the set of all sentences in the test suite, and define subsets V and A as follow:

$$V = \{s \in S \mid \text{verb}(s) = \text{sadness}\}$$

$$A = \{s \in S \mid \text{adverb}(s) = \text{joy}\}$$

The required test case would be $s' \in V \cap A$. To generate the missing test case s', we utilize:

$$s' = \text{LLM}(\text{“Generate a sentence with a verb labeled as sadness}$$

$$\text{and an adverb labeled as joy”})$$

This approach ensures that the generated sentence s' fills the identified gap in the test suite, thereby increasing the coverage of the test suite according to our proposed criteria. By adding s' to S, we obtain an augmented test suite S':

$$S' = S \cup \{s'\}$$

The augmented test suite S' now includes sentences that exhibit the desired feature combinations, leading to a more comprehensive evaluation of the model's capabilities. Additionally, as stated in the evaluation report, these types of situations might occur in user experiences and are viewed as real-life scenarios [13]. Therefore, it is crucial to include these generated tests in the test set that showcases these real-life, uncovered scenarios.

For the purpose of generating test cases, we selected the Claude language model [2] due to its capacity to generate varied and innovative test sets that are in line with our research goals. This model's attributes enable the generation of test cases that meet research requirements and highlight the robustness and reliability of sentiment analysis.

The generated sentences lack an emotion label, making them unsuitable for use as a test. To assign labels to the generated tests, we utilized six of the most accurate sentiment analysis models[1] with their accuracy mentioned in Table 1. The input sentences were fed into these models for labeling, and the resulting labels were multiplied by their accuracy on the dataset (coefficient). The sentiment with the highest score was assigned as the label for each generated sentence, a method known as "Differential Testing" [10]. The system under test was then evaluated using a combination of original and newly generated tests to assess its accuracy on the updated test set.

[1] The models used are: `bert-base-uncased-emotion` https://huggingface.co/bert-base-uncased-emotion, `bertweet-base-finetuned-emotion` https://huggingface.co/bertweet-base-finetuned-emotion, `roberta-base-emotion` https://huggingface.co/roberta-base-emotion, `xtremedistil-emotion` https://huggingface.co/xtremedistil-emotion, `sagemaker-roberta-base-emotion` https://huggingface.co/sagemaker-roberta-base-emotion, and `bertweet-emotion-base` https://huggingface.co/bertweet-emotion-base.

Table 1. Model performances under the same dataset

Model	Accuracy	Precision	Loss
roberta-base-emotion	0.931	0.936	0.152
bert-base-uncased-emotion	0.926	0.927	0.173
bertweet-base-finetuned-emotion	0.929	0.928	0.182
xtremedistil-emotion	0.926	0.928	0.226
bertweet-emotion-base	0.928	0.929	0.135
sagemaker-roberta-base-emotion	0.931	0.934	0.174

3 Experimental Results and Discussion

The dataset utilized for assessing the results is denoted as *CARER* [16]. This dataset contains six primary emotions expressed through text, enabling a thorough assessment of the neural network's ability to accurately classify emotions. The dataset is split into training and testing sets. The training set comprises 16,000 tweets, each associated with six output labels. Similarly, the test set consists of 2,000 tweets, each labeled with six output categories. A total of 18,000 tweets are chosen as the test set and assessed using the proposed coverage evaluation method. This decision was driven by the shortage of data required to achieve full coverage of the input space, particularly given the exponential growth of possible feature combinations in emotional sentiment analysis. For this study, the dataset is divided into smaller subsets, each consisting of 200 tweets, to analyze the coverage capability of each subset. Additional tests will be set based on the uncovered features.

Our model is compared to the existing test dataset since, based on our findings, no other model conducts test generation for neural networks in text categorization in the same way. This study applied the Claude language model [2] for test generation and 6 sentiment analysis models for differential testing see footnote 1. A distinct arrangement of the *DISTILBERT* model [17] was employed for word-level analysis. The process of learning and loading was executed on Google Colab, utilizing a central processing unit (CPU) with a capacity of 12.7 gigabytes of random access memory (RAM).

We tried different values of k in our implementation to evaluate the effect of k in our approach. The results presented in Fig. 1 illustrate the differences in coverage among various implementations of k. When $k = 2$, the coverage increases on average by 14% (Fig. 1a). However, when $k = 3$, the average increase in coverage is 18% (Fig. 1b). The initial coverage for $k = 3$ is 32%, while the initial coverage for $k = 2$ is 62%. This indicates that the test suite lacks sufficient coverage for complicated sentences that involve three combinations of features. Although full coverage was not attained, the sentences generated noticeably raised the total test coverage in comparison to the original data.

Figure 2 demonstrates a decline in accuracy of system under test for both test generation implementations, suggesting that the generated tests expose previ-

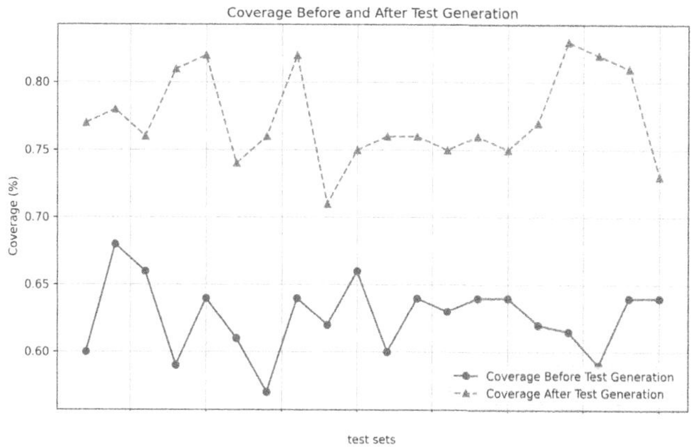

(a) Impact of Test Case Generation on Coverage for k=2

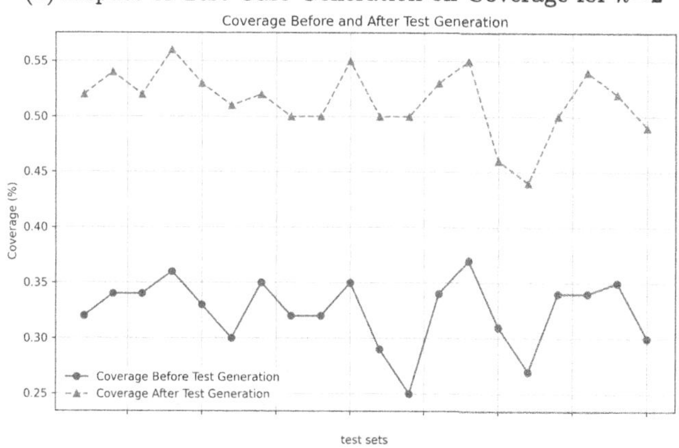

(b) Impact of Test Case Generation on Coverage for k=3

Fig. 1. Coverage comparison for k=2 and k=3

ously unexplored areas and have the potential to improve the model's functionality. When k=2 (Fig. 2a), the accuracy experiences an average loss of 5%, whereas for $k = 3$ (Fig. 2b), there is an average decrease of 8%. These findings indicate that the tests created for $k = 3$ demonstrate a higher number of defects in the model's decision-making capabilities.

The average accuracy after test generation for $k = 3$ models is 85%, whereas for $k = 2$ models it is 88%, which is lower than the model's accuracy on the base test suite, which is 94%. This indicates a decrease in the model's precision when tested on these more challenging data points. This drop results from intentionally pushing the model to its limits to uncover areas for enhancement. Based on the experimental results, $k = 3$ the augmented test suite exhibits a greater decrease in accuracy compared to $k = 2$. This can be attributed primarily to the production of more intricate sentence structures. Nevertheless, when $k = 3$,

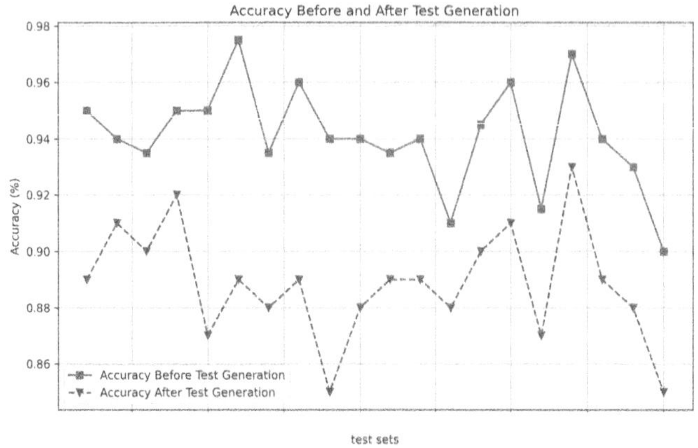

(a) Impact of Test Case Generation on Accuracy for k=2

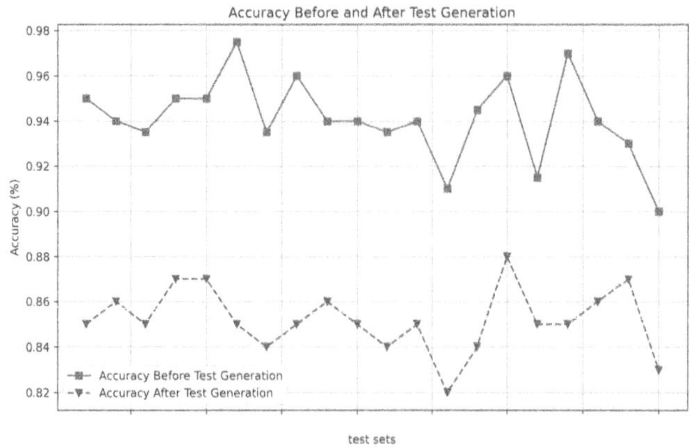

(b) Impact of Test Case Generation on Accuracy for k=3

Fig. 2. Accuracy comparison for k=2 and k=3

there is a greater time complexity and increased costs involved in generating these sentences. The sentences produced for $k = 3$ exhibit a significant level of complexity and deviate considerably from real-life situations, thereby making it challenging to evaluate the model's performance in practical settings.

To promote transparency and encourage further research, we have made the source code, datasets, and detailed replication instructions available in our GitHub repository.[2] Researchers and practitioners are invited to utilize, modify, and extend our work, and we welcome contributions and feedback to improve the methodologies and applications presented.

[2] The source code is available at https://github.com/parsakarbasi/sentiment-analysis-testing.

4 Conclusion and Future Works

This study introduced novel coverage criteria for evaluating test suites of transformer-based sentiment analysis neural networks. By using input space partitioning focused on emotionally relevant linguistic features and the k-projection coverage metric, we efficiently developed test cases and analyzed key feature subsets. Our test generation methodology, guided by the proposed coverage criteria, led to a 16% average improvement in test coverage, alongside a 6.5% reduction in model accuracy on augmented tests.

Future work could extend our coverage criteria to other transformer-based NLP tasks like text summarization or machine translation. Expanding linguistic elements beyond verbs, adjectives, adverbs, and nouns could improve the detection of subtle emotional nuances, including negations and emojis. Finally, investigating the scalability and efficiency of our methodology on larger datasets and wider applications will be essential for real-world, industry-scale applications.

References

1. Aghababaeyan, Z., et al.: Black-box testing of deep neural networks through test case diversity. IEEE Trans. Software Eng. **49**, 3182–3204 (2023)
2. Anthropic: Claude 3 (2023). https://www.anthropic.com artificial Intelligence Model
3. Bird, S.: Nltk: the natural language toolkit. In: Proceedings of the COLING/ACL 2006 Interactive Presentation Sessions, pp. 69–72 (2006)
4. Brown, T., et al.: Language models are few-shot learners. arXiv preprint (2020)
5. Chen, P.H.: Essential elements of natural language processing: what the radiologist should know. Acad. Radiol. **27**(1), 6–12 (2020)
6. Cheng, C.-H., Huang, C.-H., Yasuoka, H.: Quantitative projection coverage for testing ml-enabled autonomous systems. In: Lahiri, S.K., Wang, C. (eds.) ATVA 2018. LNCS, vol. 11138, pp. 126–142. Springer, Cham (2018). https://doi.org/10.1007/978-3-030-01090-4_8
7. Ekman, P.: An argument for basic emotions. Cognition Emotion **6**(3–4), 169–200 (1992). https://doi.org/10.1080/02699939208411068
8. Frankl, P.G., Weyuker, E.J.: An applicable family of data flow testing criteria. IEEE Trans. Software Eng. **14**(10), 1483–1498 (1988)
9. Henard, C., et al.: Comparing white-box and black-box test prioritization. In: ICSE (2016)
10. Herbold, S., Tunkel, S.: Differential testing for machine learning: an analysis for classification algorithms beyond deep learning. Empir. Softw. Eng. **28**(2), 1–18 (2023)
11. Hoffmann, J., et al.: Training compute-optimal large language models. arXiv preprint (2022)
12. Kim, J., Feldt, R., et al.: Guiding deep learning system testing using surprise adequacy. In: ICSE, pp. 1039–1049 (2019)
13. Li, Z., et al.: Structural coverage criteria for neural networks could be misleading. In: ICSE-NIER, pp. 89–92 (2019)

14. Ma, L., et al.: Deepgauge: multi-granularity testing criteria for deep learning systems. In: Proceedings of the 33rd ACM/IEEE International Conference on Automated Software Engineering, pp. 120–131 (2018)
15. Myers, G.J., Sandler, C., Carroll, T.: The Art of Software Testing, 4th edn. John Wiley & Sons (2016)
16. Saravia, E., et al.: Carer: contextualized affect representations for emotion recognition. In: Empirical Methods in Natural Language Processing, pp. 3687–3697 (2018)
17. Savani, B.: Distilbert-base-uncased-emotion - a fine-tuned distilbert model for emotion classification (2023). https://huggingface.co/bhadresh-savani/distilbert-base-uncased-emotion
18. Thoppilan, R., et al.: Lamda: Language models for dialog applications. arXiv preprint (2022)
19. Vaswani, A., et al.: Attention is all you need. In: Advances in Neural Information Processing Systems, pp. 599–609 (2017)

Machine Learning and Large Language Models

Automating Invariant Filtering: Leveraging LLMs to Streamline Test Oracle Generation

Stefan Fischer(✉) and Claus Klammer

Software Competence Center Hagenberg GmbH (SCCH), Hagenberg, Austria
{stefan.fischer,claus.klammer}@scch.at

Abstract. Automated generation of test oracles is a critical area of research in software quality assurance. One effective technique is the detection of invariants by analyzing dynamic execution data. Though a common challenge of these approaches is the detection of *false-positive* invariants. This paper investigates the potential of Large Language Models (LLMs) to assist in filtering these dynamically detected invariants, aiming to reduce the manual effort involved in discarding incorrect invariants. We conducted experiments using various GPT models from OpenAI, leveraging a dataset of invariants detected from the dynamic execution of REST APIs. By employing a *Zero-shot Chain-of-Thought Prompting* methodology, we guided the LLMs to articulate their reasoning behind their decisions. Our findings indicate that classification performance improves with detailed instructions and strategic prompt design (the best model achieving on average 80.7% accuracy), with some performance differences between different invariant types.

Keywords: Test Oracle · Constraint-Mining · Invariant-Detection · Large-Language-Models

1 Introduction

Automated generation of test oracles is an active research area aimed at improving software quality assurance. Various methods, including machine learning techniques [4,14,17], evolutionary algorithms [13], or statistical data analysis [1,5], have been applied to this domain. A common approach for test oracle generation involves the detection of likely invariants-properties of a program that should always hold true during execution [1,5]. Dynamic approaches that discover invariants by analyzing program inputs and outputs are particularly appealing, as they can be applied in a variety of contexts. However, a significant challenge associated with these approaches is the detection of *false-positive* invariants, which may only hold for the specific dataset used for inference and fail in broader execution contexts. This leads to considerable manual effort in filtering these detected invariants, creating a hurdle to practical application.

J. Fischbach et al. (Eds.): SWQD 2025, LNBIP 544, pp. 51–71, 2025.
https://doi.org/10.1007/978-3-031-89277-6_4

Recent advancements in Artificial Intelligence, particularly in the field of Natural Language Processing, have led to the emergence of Large Language Models (LLMs). These models, have demonstrated their ability to understand and generate human-like text, making them promising candidates for automating complex tasks in software engineering [9,10]. This includes their application in a large variety of software testing tasks [16].

This paper investigates the potential of LLMs to classify dynamically detected invariants as either *true-positives* or *false-positives*, thereby reducing the manual effort required in invariant filtering. Our experiments utilize a set of invariants detected from dynamic data generated during automated testing on Representational State Transfer (REST) APIs. We employed various GPT models developed by OpenAI, providing them with specific instructions to assess the invariants accordingly. For each invariant, we generated a prompt that includes an excerpt from the OpenAPI specification of the REST API, the textual representation of the invariant, and a description of the invariant by type. We detail our process for enhancing the instructions provided to the LLMs and the prompts tailored for individual invariants, along with other strategies aimed at improving classification results.

Our approach employs a *Zero-shot Chain-of-Thought Prompting* methodology, which encourages the LLMs to articulate their reasoning processes when making classifications. We found that this methodology, combined with effective prompt engineering, yields promising results for classification performance of the LLMs, thereby offering valuable insights into their applicability in automating invariant filtering. Our work seeks to contribute to the ongoing exploration of AI applications in software quality assurance. Ultimately, we aim to demonstrate how LLMs can alleviate the burden of manual verification in invariant detection, facilitating a broader adoption of invariant detection techniques.

2 Background and Related Work

In this section we summarize the necessary background to our work and outline the most important related work.

2.1 Invariant Detection

Program invariants play a crucial role in formal verification, debugging, and software testing by providing additional specifications that can be automatically checked. However, many software systems lack these specifications, and those supplied by programmers are often outdated, ineffective, or incorrect [5,13]. To address this gap, various techniques have been developed to automatically detect invariants. These techniques are broadly categorized into two main types: static and dynamic invariant detection.

Static invariant detection involves analyzing source code, documentation, or program specifications. For example, approaches infer assertions by analyzing source code using machine learning techniques [4,17]. Gay et al. use behavioral models as program specifications, which they automatically refine to align more closely with actual system behavior [6]. On the other hand, Blasi et al. combine pattern matching, lexical analysis, and semantic techniques to translate Javadoc comments into formal procedure specifications [2]. Similarly, Goffi et al. use natural language processing techniques to derive conditions for exceptional program behaviors from Javadoc comments [8]. Although static analysis is thorough and typically results in highly accurate invariants, it can be conservative, identifying fewer invariants compared to dynamic methods. Furthermore, static techniques may face scalability challenges when applied to large or complex systems due to computational limitations.

In contrast, dynamic invariant detection relies on analyzing execution data to identify invariants based on real program runs. One prominent example is Daikon, a tool that detects likely invariants by observing program executions [5]. Daikon instruments the program and tracks variable values across executions, supporting languages such as C, C++, C#, Eiffel, F#, Java, Perl, and Visual Basic. Recent work by Alonso et al. extends Daikon to detect invariants in REST APIs [1]. Another approach by Molina et al. generates program executions for Java methods and applies a genetic algorithm to identify post-conditions that hold at the end of method executions [13]. While dynamic techniques can discover more nuanced, data-driven invariants, they are prone to generating *false-positives*, especially when the execution data lacks sufficient variety [1,5].

2.2 LLMs in Software Engineering

LLMs have gained significant traction in various software engineering tasks, providing automation, analysis, and classification capabilities across a wide range of domains [9,10]. In software testing, LLMs support tasks like test case and oracle generation, defect detection, and bug analysis [16]. For example, Lee et al. use LLMs to classify logical errors in programs into different types, showing how *GPT-4* achieved up to 86% accuracy in identifying these errors [12]. Vito et al. applied LLMs to classify issue reports, helping developers focus on the most critical problems [15]. Similarly, Chuor et al. used LLMs to classify user stories, which enhances requirement management and prioritization efforts in agile development [3]. Kim at al. investigated the use of LLMs to enhance OpenAPI specifications with additional machine-readable constraints mined from the contained natural language descriptions, to support automated test generation [11].

The success of LLMs in software engineering often hinges on the prompting techniques used to guide their outputs. Various prompting strategies have emerged, such as *Chain-of-Thought Prompting*, where the model reasons step by step, improving performance on complex tasks. *Instruction-based Prompting* provides clear task instructions, while *Zero-shot Prompting* asks the model to perform a task without examples, relying on its pre-trained knowledge. *One-shot* and *Few-shot Prompting* provide one or a few examples of the desired responses to help the model generalize better [9].

As LLMs can sometimes generate unreliable outputs, assessing their confidence helps mitigate risks and improve reliability [7]. Confidence estimation techniques include *logit-based* methods, which assess token-level probabilities (e.g., minimum or average token probability, entropy), and *linguistic* confidence, where models express uncertainty through human-readable terms (e.g., "low," "medium," "high") or numerical scores. Xiong et al. explored how *linguistic* confidence can provide additional reliability insights for LLM outputs [18].

3 Problem Statement

Dynamic invariant detection techniques often generate a significant number of *false-positives*, especially when the program's executions under analysis lack sufficient variety [1]. Failing to address these incorrect invariants can lead to misleading system behavior during program verification or testing, where such invariants may cause valid executions to be falsely flagged as failures, despite the program behaving as intended. Consequently, the output from dynamic invariant detectors requires manual filtering by human experts to eliminate these spurious results [5]. However, given that the number of detected invariants can easily reach into the thousands for complex systems, this manual filtering process becomes labor-intensive, time-consuming, and costly. Our work aims to tackle this challenge by automating the filtering of incorrect invariants, thereby reducing the human effort required and lowering the overhead involved in using dynamic invariant detection approaches.

4 Method

For our experiments, we rely on data from a study that presents the *AGORA* approach for detecting invariants in REST APIs [1]. At the core of this approach is an adapted version of the *Daikon* invariant detector, which has been extended with additional *invariant types* specifically designed to better suit the unique characteristics of REST APIs. To generate the execution data necessary for invariant detection, the authors employed an automated REST test generation approach, producing up to $10,000$ valid requests and responses (i.e., those returning a $2XX$ response code). Specifically, they performed their experiments with 50, 100, 500, $1,000$, and $10,000$ API calls, with both the original *Daikon invariant types* and the adapted *AGORA* ones. The authors provide a comprehensive replication package, which includes data on the detected invariants labeled as *true-positive* or *false-positive*, the OpenAPI specifications of the tested API operations, and the test data used during invariant detection. We summarize the invariant data from their study in Table 1. Their experiments were conducted on eleven API operations across seven publicly available systems. We aggregated the invariant data for all their experiments with different numbers of API calls and invariant settings. In total, their approach detected $1,731$ invariants, which contain labels as either *true-positives* or *false-positives* based on whether the invariants accurately described the behavior of the corresponding API. This labeling resulted in 869 *true-positives* (correct invariants) and 862 *false-positives* (incorrect invariants). The availability of this manually labeled dataset provides a strong baseline for our experiments, and the data played a crucial role in shaping the design of our experiments.

Table 1. Invariant data used for our experiments, provided by [1]

API - Operation	Detected Invariants		
	true-positive	false-positive	SUM
AmadeusHotel-getMultiHotelOffers	83	193	276
GitHub-createOrganizationRepository	200	4	204
GitHub-getOrganizationRepositories	137	36	173
Marvel-getComicById	101	218	319
OMDB-byIdOrTitle	15	4	19
OMDB-bySearch	8	3	11
Spotify-createPlaylist	48	0	48
Spotify-getAlbumTracks	65	38	103
Spotify-getArtistAlbums	56	31	87
Yelp-getBusinesses	24	65	89
YouTube-listVideos	132	270	402
TOTAL	869	862	1731

Table 2. Invariant data by invariant category

Invariant Category	Detected Invariants		
	true-positive	false-positive	SUM
Arithmetic comparisons	176	636	812
Array properties	35	98	133
Specific formats	306	14	320
Specific values	124	93	217
String comparisons	228	21	249

Alonso et al. include 34 *invariant types* in their study. An *invariant type* represents a general invariant pattern that can be instantiated for specific data fields to generate applicable invariants. For example, *invariant type* `isURL(String)` can be instantiated to a specific invariant, by applying it to a string field and verify whether it conforms to a URL format. These *invariant types* are organized into five broader categories based on the properties they check and the types of values they compare [1]. Table 2 shows the number of invariants in each category, along with the counts of those labeled as *true-positive* and *false-positive*. This distinction is of interest to us as well, because LLMs might perform different based on the type of invariant.

Figure 1 illustrates the workflow of our experiments. A key aspect of the process is ensuring clear communication with the LLM, which involves providing precise instructions for the task and passing the necessary data for it to accurately classify invariants. To accomplish this, we send two messages to the LLM. The first is the *System Message* (sent with OpenAI's role *system*), which provides instructions on the task and explains how the LLM should evaluate different invariants. The second message, the *Prompt* (sent with OpenAI's role *user*), includes detailed information about the API and the specific invariant being evaluated. The *Prompt* is automatically generated using available data, such as the OpenAPI specification, the string representation of the invariant, the type of invariant, along with a description of the invariant type based on the *Daikon* and *AGORA* documentations. Additionally, we provide examples of the data on which the invariant was detected to give the LLM further context for evaluation. We utilized the function calling feature of the OpenAI API to ensure the LLM returns responses in a structured format, as JSON objects. This enables automated post-processing of classification outputs, allowing for a more efficient evaluation

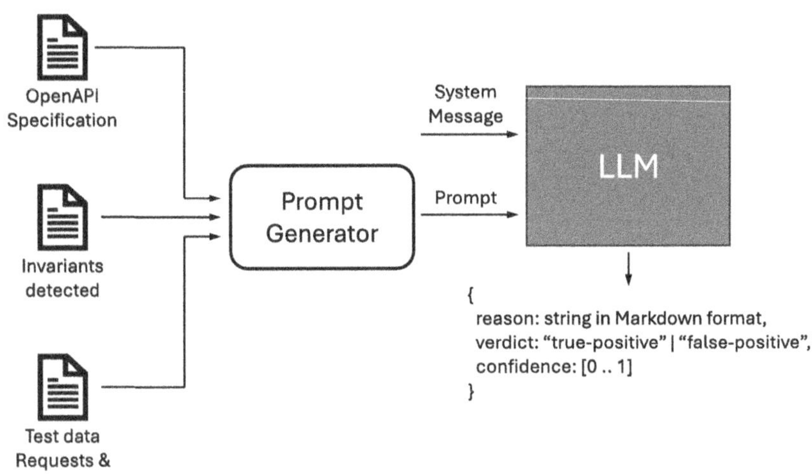

Fig. 1. Overview of the method for our experiments

We incrementally improved our prompting to achieve better results. To outline this, we will now discuss two major setups, with different messages and data passed to the LLMs.

4.1 Initial Setup: Simple System Message and Static Prompts

As outlined earlier, we provide the LLM with two key messages: *(i)* the *System Message*, which instructs the LLM to act as an assistant responsible for determining whether an invariant holds or not, and *(ii)* the *Prompt*, which contains details about the specific invariant along with the corresponding excerpt from the OpenAPI specification. Figure 2 displays the *System Message*. Importantly, we instruct the LLM to include a reasoning explanation for its invariant classification. This approach leverages *Chain-of-Thought Prompting*, which has been shown to improve performance in reasoning tasks for LLMs by guiding them to articulate their thought process step by step.

```
You are an assistant that evaluates if a given invariant is correct for a REST API.
Your task is to classify the invariant as "true-positive" (i.e., correct: holds for
every valid request on the API) or "false-positive" (i.e., incorrect: will not hold
for every valid request on the API) and provide your reasoning for the decision.
```

Fig. 2. System message to instruct the LLM about its task.

```
Is the following invariant for a REST endpoint "true-positive" or "false-positive"?

This is an excerpt of the swagger definition:

paths:
  "/shopping/hotel-offers"
  get:
    summary: getMultiHotelOffers
    parameters:
    responses:
      '200': ...
        data: ...
          offers: ...
            price: ...
              taxes: ...
                type: array
                items:
                  pricingFrequency:
                    type: string
                    description: Specifies if the tax applies per stay or per night
                                 - PER_STAY
                                 - PER_NIGHT


Is the following invariant a true-positive or a false-positive:
Invariant: "return.pricingFrequency one of { ""PER_NIGHT"", ""PER_STAY"" }"

Invariant type: daikon.inv.unary.string.OneOfString
Invariant description: Represents String variables that take on only a few distinct values. Prints as either
       x == c (when there is only one value) or as x one of {c1, c2, c3} (when there are multiple values).
Fields starting with "input" are request parameters or fields in the request body.
Fields starting with "return" are fields in the response body.
The return fields refer to the path "data.offers.price.taxes" in the response body.
```

Listing 1.1. *Prompt* to classify an invariant for *AmadeusHotel-getMultiHotelOffers*

The *Prompt Generator* carries out several tasks to prepare input for the LLMs. First, it extracts the input and return variables from each invariant, using them to pull relevant excerpts from the OpenAPI specification. This step is crucial, as the full OpenAPI specifications for the API operations are too large to pass to the LLMs in their entirety, which would cause a context overflow. We generate a simplified YAML string for the OpenAPI specification, containing only the information necessary to evaluate the invariant. For each variable, we include its data type and the description provided in the OpenAPI specification. Additionally, if available, we also include examples of variable values, patterns for string values, minimum or maximum value lengths, and any enumeration values that the variable can take. Each invariant in the dataset is associated with one of 34 distinct *invariant types*. To provide more detail about the invariant being classified, we include a description of its type, which we extract from the *Daikon* documentation or, for invariants added by [1], from the *AGORA* documentation. Listing 1.1 shows an example of a generated *Prompt* for the API operation *AmadeusHotel-getMultiHotelOffers*. For conciseness, we omitted some details of the API specification excerpt, indicated by the placeholder "..″ in the listing. In this example, the invariant restricts the value of a response variable to one of two possible values, which is confirmed by the variable's description in the OpenAPI specification. This case highlights the advantage of using an LLM for classification, as the confirmation of the invariant relies on interpreting the natural language description within the variable's specification-a task well-suited for language models.

To ensure structured and consistent responses from the LLM, we utilized the function calling feature of the OpenAI API. This allows us to define the exact structure in which the LLM returns its output, which is critical for automated processing of the results. The response is designed to include two main properties: *reason* and *verdict*. The *reason* property is contained to further enforce the *Chain-of-Thought Prompting* by passing the steps the reasoning should contain with the following description: `Contains the complete reasoning about the decision in markdown including sections ‘‘Swagger Definition Breakdown’’, ‘‘Invariant’’, ‘‘Analysis’’, ‘‘Conclusion’’.` The *verdict* property contains the classification of the invariant, with the following description: `The verdict on the invariant, can be ‘‘true-positive’’ or ‘‘false-positive’’.`

Listing 1.2 shows an example for a *reason* response, given by *GPT-4o-mini*, to the *System Message* in Fig. 2 and the *Prompt* in Listing 1.1. We can see that the reasoning follows the steps we specified and comes to the correct conclusion that the invariant is *true-positive*.

```
### Swagger Definition Breakdown
The provided Swagger definition describes a GET endpoint for retrieving hotel offers. The response schema
indicates that the response will contain an object with a property ‘data‘, which is an array of offers. Each
 offer contains a ‘price‘ object, which in turn contains a ‘taxes‘ array. Each item in the ‘taxes‘ array is
expected to have a ‘pricingFrequency‘ property that specifies how the tax applies.

### Invariant
The invariant states that the ‘pricingFrequency‘ must be one of the two specified values: "PER_NIGHT" or "
PER_STAY". This is a common pattern for fields that have a limited set of acceptable values.

### Analysis
The invariant is based on the description provided in the Swagger definition, which explicitly states that
the ‘pricingFrequency‘ can take on the values "PER_STAY" or "PER_NIGHT". Since the schema defines these as
the only possible values for the ‘pricingFrequency‘ property, the invariant holds true for every valid
response from the API. There are no other values mentioned or implied in the schema that would contradict
this invariant.

### Conclusion
Given that the Swagger definition clearly specifies the allowed values for ‘pricingFrequency‘, the invariant
 is correct and holds for every valid request on the API. Therefore, the invariant is classified as a **true
-positive**.
```

Listing 1.2. Reasoning response for the invariant classification

After first experiments with this setup, we found the results not to our satisfaction and therefore improved on the *Prompt* and the *System Message*.

4.2 Enhanced Setup: Improved System Message and Data Examples

To improve our results, we began by revisiting the *System Message* and adding more detailed instructions on how to classify the invariants. This follows the principles of *Instruction-based Prompting*, which emphasizes providing clearer and more specific guidance on how the LLM should complete a task [9]. Figure 3 shows the updated *System Message* for our experiments. The improvements include several key changes:

- **Confidence Assessment:** We instructed the LLM to evaluate and report its confidence level in each classification, as an attempt to provide a likelihood on how reliable the classification might be.
- **Execution Data Information:** We added details about the number of API requests used to derive the invariants and instructed the LLM to consider the amount of empirical data supporting an invariant, as more data typically increases the likelihood of a correct invariant.
- **Classification instructions:** We included more explicit instructions on when an invariant is more likely to be classified as a *true-positive* or *false-positive*. For instance, in the initial experiment, invariants involving string-type variables performed notably poorly as many correct invariants were discarded. To address this, we instructed the LLM to adopt a less stringent approach when evaluating these invariants.

```
You are an assistant that evaluates if a given invariant is correct for a REST API.
Your task is to classify the invariant as "true-positive" (i.e., correct: holds for
every valid request on the API) or "false-positive" (i.e., incorrect: will not hold
for every valid request on the API) and provide your reasoning for the decision and
your confidence how sure you are about the classification.
We tried from 50 up to 10000 calls for the operation to find different invariants.
If we have tried more calls and found more examples of the invariant holding it
should be regarded more likely that the invariant is a "true-positive".
If there is an invariant on a string variable, for which we have many examples or
calls, that might make sense and the specification does not clearly contradict the
invariant, it should be regarded as a likely "true-positive".
If the invariant restricts the value of a variable and the specification explicitly
mentions other values the variable can take on, it is most likely a "false-positive".
You should also consider the semantics of the variables in the context of the
invariant. For instance, if we compare two variables where it makes no semantic
sense, the invariant is most likely a "false-positive".
```

Fig. 3. Improved System message with more instructions for classification.

Next, we adapted the *Prompt Generator* to enrich the information provided to the LLM. Specifically, we added details about the number of API calls supporting the invariant and the number of example variable values from the execution data, including how many were distinct. Up to five random distinct examples of variable values were included, excluding those with string representations exceeding 200 characters to avoid overloading the LLM context. Unlike *Few-shot Prompting*, which provides examples of expected responses, we provided examples of the input data used to infer the invariant. Listing 1.3 shows the additional information added to the *Prompt* from Listing 1.1. In this case, we found two distinct variable values and included both in the *Prompt* for the LLM to consider.

```
...

We have tried 10000 calls on this API and did not find a single counter example.

We found 22609 examples in the requests data, with 2 of them being distinct examples.
Here are 2 example values of the variables:
output.data.offers.price.taxes.pricingFrequency=PER_STAY
output.data.offers.price.taxes.pricingFrequency=PER_NIGHT
```

Listing 1.3. Improved *Prompt* with number of calls and example data

The final adaptation we made to enhance our results was the addition of a *confidence* property to the structured response. This instructed the LLM to assess and report its confidence in the classification verdict. We used the following description for this property: `The confidence about the verdict, as a number between 0 and 1 (0 very low confidence, 1 very high confidence)`. This approach is inspired by the work of Xiong et al., who prompted LLMs to express uncertainty about their answers by providing a confidence value for each response [18]. By incorporating confidence assessment, we aimed to provide a more nuanced understanding of the LLM's decision-making process, allowing us to gauge the reliability of its classifications.

4.3 Experiment Execution and Evaluation

We aggregated the invariants from the original experiments by API operation, combining all invariants over the different number of API calls and derived with the original *Daikon invariant types* and the adapted ones implemented in *AGORA*. This left us with a dataset of 1731 labeled invariants, as outlined in Table 1. For each invariant we have as data available the string representation of the invariant, its *invariant type*, the list of variables that are involved, and the label (*true-positive* or *false-positive*). Moreover, for each API operation we have the OpenAPI specification and the execution data that was used to infer the invariants in [1].

We performed the first experiments, with the initial setup as described in Sect. 4.1, using the OpenAI GPT models: *GPT-3.5* (``gpt-3.5-turbo-1106'') and *GPT-4o-mini* (``gpt-4o-mini-2024-07-18''). After analyzing these first results we found slightly better results for *GPT-3.5* compared to *GPT-4o-mini*. However, *GPT-4o-mini* achieved better results for *Precision* and the results for both models were still not to our satisfaction. Because of the higher *Precision* and the lower cost per token, we used *GPT-4o-mini* to assess further improvements and prompt engineering. After incremental changes, using only a subset of the data, we arrived at the setup described in Sect. 4.2. Subsequently, we performed the experiments with the complete data, with this setup, using *GPT-3.5*, *GPT-4o-mini* and additionally with the more expensive *GPT-4o* (``gpt-4o-2024-08-06'').

We set the *Temperature* to 0.2 for all experiments to make the output more deterministic and focused. For executing the experiments, we implemented the *Prompt Generator* and the communication with the OpenAI API in Java and executed it on a laptop with Intel i7-1365U @1.80 GHz, 16GB RAM running Windows 11 and Java 17. The Java code and all the results for our experiments can be found in our online appendix[1].

The goal of our experiments is to evaluate the performance of LLMs to filter out *false-positive* invariants without incorrectly discarding *true-positives*, thereby reducing the manual overhead required in dynamic invariant detection. To achieve this, we formulated the following five research questions:

- **RQ1:** How does the classification performance differ between the two setups? *Rationale:* We are interested in how varying the level of instruction detail and data provided to the LLM affects performance. Effective prompt engineering requires effort, especially when covering edge cases, so understanding this balance is important.
- **RQ2:** How does the classification performance differ between the different LLMs? *Rationale:* The different GPT models used in our experiments come with varying costs. It's important to determine if higher-cost models deliver significantly better performance, making them worth the additional expense.
- **RQ3:** How does the classification performance differ between the API-Operations? *Rationale:* The quality of OpenAPI specifications may vary significantly between API operations. Therefore, we want to investigate if we can find significant differences in the classification performance between them.
- **RQ4:** How does the classification performance differ between the invariant categories? *Rationale:* LLMs may not perform the same for different invariants types. Therefore, we want to analyze whether classification performance varies across different categories of invariants.
- **RQ5:** Can the LLMs' self-assessed confidence indicate the reliability of their classifications? *Rationale:* If the confidence values provided by the LLMs reflect the accuracy of their classifications, they could help prioritize which invariants require manual review. This could significantly reduce the human effort involved in filtering *false-positives*, as reviewers would only need to focus on invariants with lower confidence scores.

To measure the performance of the GPT models to classify the invariants we use common metrics for classification tasks:

- **TP:** The number of invariants the LLM ruled as *true-positive* correctly (label: *true-positive*, LLM verdict: *true-positive*).

[1] https://github.com/software-competence-center-hagenberg/2025-SWQD-LLM-Invariant-classification.

- **TN:** The number of invariants the LLM ruled as *false-positive* correctly (label: *false-positive*, LLM verdict: *false-positive*).
- **FP:** The number of invariants the LLM ruled as *true-positive* incorrectly (label: *false-positive*, LLM verdict: *true-positive*).
- **FN:** The number of invariants the LLM ruled as *false-positive* incorrectly (label: *true-positive*, LLM verdict: *false-positive*).
- **Precision** $= \frac{TP}{TP+FP}$
- **Recall** $= \frac{TP}{TP+FN}$
- **Accuracy** $= \frac{TP+TN}{TP+TN+FP+FN}$
- **F1-Score** $= \frac{2*TP}{2*TP+FP+FN}$

Additionally, we report the consumed input and output tokens for our experiments on the different LLMs and the cost associated with the token use.

5 Results

5.1 Initial Setup: Simple System Message and Static Prompts

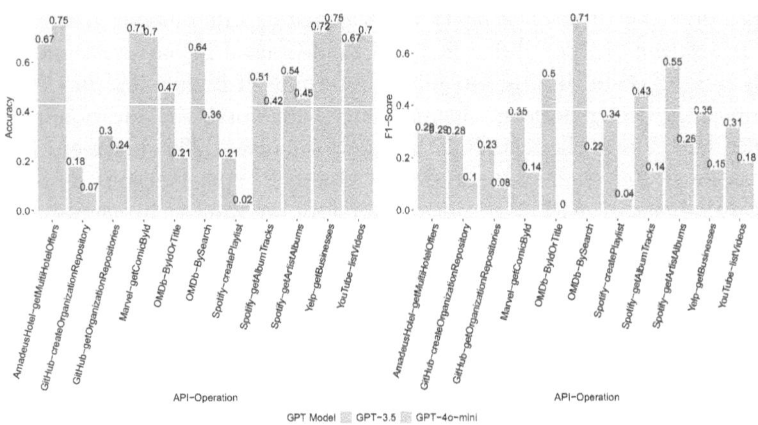

Fig. 4. Metrics per API-Operation in Setup 1

First, we present the results of our initial experiment setup, described in Sect. 4.1. We depict the results for *Accuracy* and *F1-Score* on the different API-Operations in Fig. 4. Looking at the *Accuracy* we see similar results for both LLMs. Generally, if one did better so did the other. However, in most cases *GPT-3.5* outperformed *GPT-4o-mini* here, with an average *Accuracy* of 0.56 compared to 0.54. The difference between the two models becomes more noticeable when looking at the *F1-Score*. Here *GPT-3.5* on average achieved a value of 0.34, and *GPT-4o-mini* only 0.15. Further investigating the *Precision* and *Recall* we find the reason for these different results. *GPT-4o-mini* achieved a very high

Precision of 0.95, but a *Recall* of only 0.08. This is because *GPT-4o-mini* was very strict in classifying and its *FP* count is only 4 invariants. However, its *FN* count is 800 invariants, which were discarded incorrectly, only leaving 69 (*TP*) correct invariants. On the other hand, *GPT-3.5* had a lower *Precision* of 0.67, but a better *Recall* of 0.22. However, it still discarded 674 (*FN*) correct invariants and let 96 (*FP*) incorrect invariants slip through.

The same metrics over the invariants categories can be seen in Fig. 5. We found the worst results in the categories *Specific formats* and *String comparisons.* For the *Array properties* category *GPT-4o-mini* has an *F1-Score* of zero, because it discarded all invariants leaving none in *TP.*

5.2 Enhanced Setup: Improved System Message and Data Examples

Now we present the results for our second setup, described in Sect. 4.2. Again, we depict the results for *Accuracy* and *F1-Score* on the different API-Operations, see Fig. 6. *GPT-4o-mini* performed better, compared to Setup 1, in terms of *Accuracy* (on average 0.76) and *F1-Score* (on average 0.74) in almost all cases, with the exception of the *Accuracy* for operation *Yelp-getBusinesses* being slightly better in the first setup. In sum it now discarded 288 (*FN*) correct invariants and included 129 (*FP*) incorrect ones. For *GPT-3.5* the average *Accuracy* stayed the same as in the first setup, at 0.56. However, the *F1-Score* increased to on average 0.67. In sum it now included 684 (*FP*) incorrect invariants and discarded 86 (*FN*) correct ones. The average performance for both LLMs increased, now with *GPT-4o-mini* outperforming *GPT-3.5*. However, *GPT-4o* outperforms both of them with an average *Accuracy* of 0.81 and *F1-Score* of 0.82. It included 229 (*FP*) incorrect invariants and discarded 105 (*FN*) correct ones.

For the invariant categories we found significant changes compared to the first setup, as depicted in Fig. 7. The two categories *Specific formats* and *String*

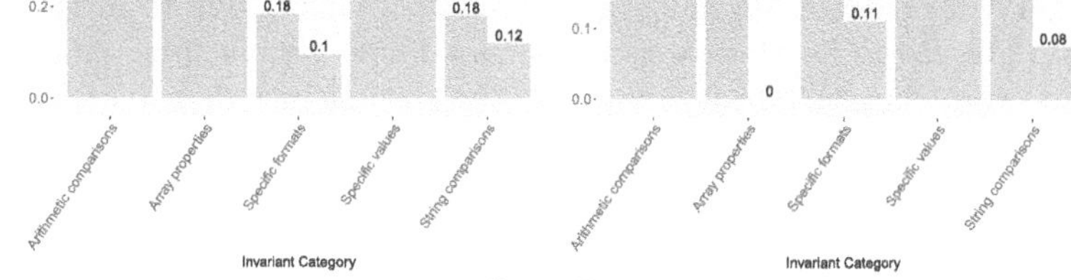

Fig. 5. Metrics per invariant category in Setup 1

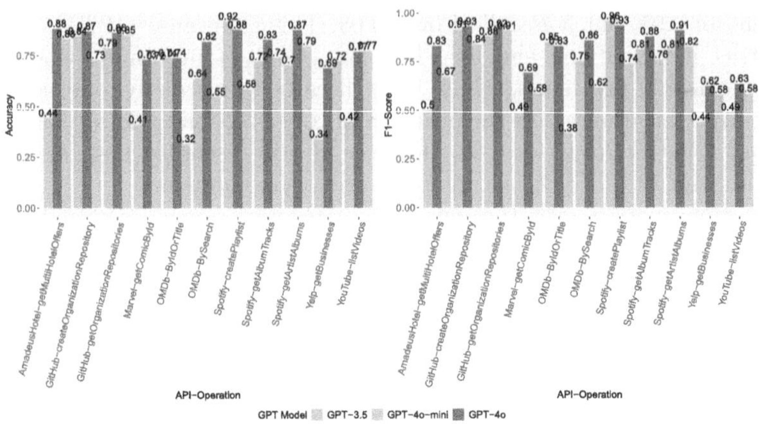

Fig. 6. Metrics per API-Operation in Setup 2

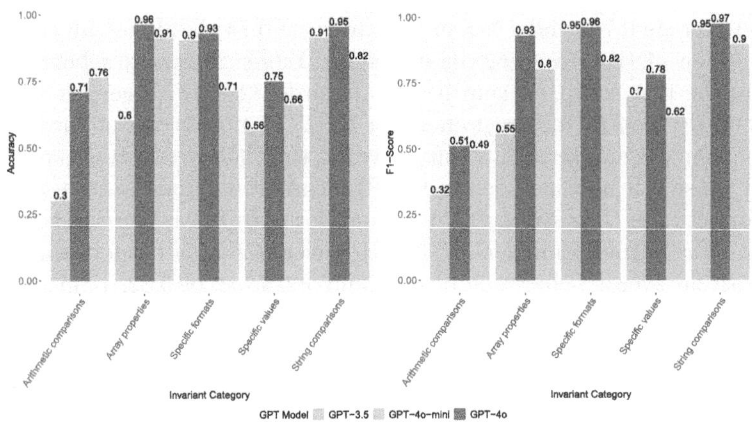

Fig. 7. Metrics per invariant category in Setup 2

comparisons, which had the worst performance in the first setup, now performed significantly better. However, the category *Arithmetic comparisons*, which had one of the best results in the first setup, now performed worse and as the weakest category in terms of *Accuracy* and *F1-Score*. This is due to a decrease in *Precision*. The *Recall* for this category increased however, meaning more correct invariants were classified *true-positive* at the cost of including more incorrect invariants.

Finally, we analyzed the values returned by the LLMs for their self-assessed confidence regarding the classification of invariants. On average, we found that for invariants classified as *true-positives*, the correct ones in *TP* had a higher confidence value than the incorrect ones in *FP*. In contrast, we did not observe such a difference in confidence values over *TN* and *FN*, for invariants classified as *false-positives*.

To further understand the relationship between confidence and classification, we conducted an ANOVA analysis focused on invariants classified as *true-positives* by the LLMs. This analysis revealed a statistically significant correlation between confidence levels and the correctness (i.e., *TP* or *FP*). However, no such relationship was found for invariants classified as *false-positives*, indicating that confidence assessments may have no utility for these cases.

To investigate the potential of using confidence to filter invariants classified as *true-positives*, we plotted the proportional distribution of invariants across specific confidence values, as shown in Fig. 8. For *GPT-3.5*, we observed that most invariants overlap significantly in their confidence values, making it challenging to apply a confidence threshold without discarding a substantial number of correct invariants. In contrast, *GPT-4o-mini* and *GPT-4o* demonstrated clearer distinctions in their confidence distributions, suggesting that a well-defined confidence threshold could effectively filter out many incorrect invariants while retaining most correct ones. Nevertheless, the majority of invariants still necessitate manual evaluation to eliminate the remaining *false-positives*.

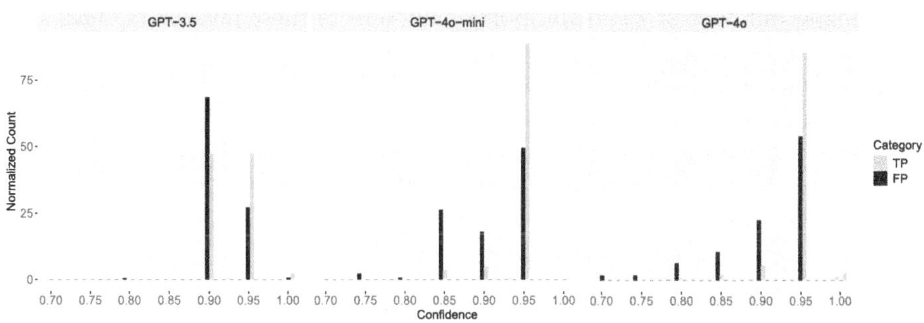

Fig. 8. Normalized histogram of the confidence given by each LLM for invariants classified as *true-positives* (i.e., *TP* and *FP*)

Table 3. Token usage in all experiments

LLM		Input Token			Output Token			Total Cost
		Total	Avg.	Cost	Total	Avg.	Cost	
Setup 1	GPT-3.5	918378	530.55	0.92$	346139	200.00	0.69$	1.61$
	GPT-4o-mini	911789	526.74	0.14$	692733	400.19	0.42$	0.56$
Setup 2	GPT-3.5	1519181	877.93	1.52$	434521	251.02	0.87$	2,39$
	GPT-4o-mini	1509784	872.20	0.23$	742215	428.78	0.45$	0.68$
	GPT-4o	1509628	872.11	3.77$	775638	448.09	7.76$	11.53$

5.3 Token Use

Here we briefly summarize the token usage and associated cost by our experiments, in total for each LLMs in the respective setup and on average per invariant (see Table 3).

6 Discussion

In this section, we discuss the outcomes of our experiments in relation to the five research questions posed.

6.1 RQ1: Difference Between Setups

Our experiments showed an increase in classification performance when utilizing the improved *System Message* and enriched *Prompt*. The detailed instructions and additional context provided to the LLMs enhanced their results overall. However, we noted a setback in the results specifically for the *Arithmetic Comparisons* category, where the performance did not meet expectations. Notably this category contains the majority of the *false-positives* in the original data and a higher number of *FP* disproportionally affects these invariants. This suggests that while the second setup yielded overall improvements, certain invariant categories may still pose challenges. Nevertheless, the effort invested in prompt engineering proved beneficial, as evidenced by the enhanced results in other categories. It is plausible that the subpar performance in the *Arithmetic Comparisons* category could be mitigated through further refinement of the instructions, indicating an opportunity for ongoing optimization in our approach.

6.2 RQ2: Difference Between LLMs

Our analysis of the different LLMs revealed that each model had its own strengths across various metrics. Notably, *GPT-3.5* excelled in *Recall*, but was the worst in *Precision*. On the other hand, *GPT-4o-mini* demonstrated superior *Precision*, suggesting it was more discerning in its classifications and included fewer *false-positives*. However, *GPT-4o* emerged as the standout model overall, achieving the highest *Accuracy* and *F1-Score*. This suggests that while different models may be optimized for specific performance metrics, *GPT-4o* provided the most balanced performance across the board. These results suggest that combining these models could be beneficial to capitalize on their respective strengths and weaknesses. For instance, while *GPT-4o-mini* offers high *Precision*, it has lower *Recall*, meaning the invariants it classifies as *true-positives* are more likely to be correct. In contrast, the invariants classified as *true-positives* only by *GPT-3.5* and *GPT-4o* may require additional human evaluation, as they could encompass more *false-positives*. Therefore, a mixed approach utilizing multiple models could enhance overall classification reliability and efficiency.

Additionally, we noted that the responses by *GPT-4o-mini* and *GPT-4o* contained more detailed reasoning compared to *GPT-3.5*. *GPT-4o-mini* and *GPT-4o* did provide more explanations in breaking down the OpenAPI specification, the invariant and the analysis of their conformance or contradiction. This is also visible in the number of output tokens produced in Table 3.

6.3 RQ3: Difference Between API-Operations

To investigate the influence of different *API-Operations* and *invariant types* on classification performance, we conducted an ANOVA analysis focused on both *Accuracy* and *F1-Score*. Our results indicated statistical significance for the *invariant type*, suggesting that the classification performance varies based on the specific characteristics of the invariants. However, we did not find statistically significant differences attributable to the *API-Operations*.

To further understand the impact of *invariant type*, we assessed the effect size using Cohen's f^2 and Partial η^2. This analysis revealed a stronger effect size for *invariant type* across both performance metrics, confirming its substantial influence on the classification outcomes. Additionally, we performed feature extraction using a random forest model, which corroborated the higher effect of *invariant type* on performance.

Despite the overarching trends, we also examined specific performance differences within certain *invariant categories* across various *API-Operations*. Our analysis highlighted that variations in OpenAPI specifications could significantly impact the LLM's ability to accurately classify invariants. For example, the level of detail in the natural language descriptions provided in the specifications, or even the absence of descriptions, can hinder the LLM's performance. Furthermore, additional factors such as the presence of examples, patterns, and length restrictions within the specifications were found to influence classification effectiveness.

6.4 RQ4: Difference Between Invariant Categories

As previously noted, our analysis revealed a strong correlation between classification performance and the various *invariant types*. It is evident that invariant classification does not yield uniform results across different *categories*. However, the performance differences observed between our two setups underscore the significance of prompt engineering in addressing the shortcomings present in certain categories.

Notably, the tailored instructions regarding invariants associated with string-type variables had a substantial impact on improving results, particularly in the categories of *Specific formats* and *String comparisons*. This enhancement illustrates how focused prompt adjustments can mitigate specific challenges within invariant classification.

Despite these improvements, our correlation analysis confirmed that the strongest relationship lies between *invariant type* and classification performance.

This indicates a clear disparity in performance across different categories, highlighting the need for targeted strategies in handling specific invariant types to optimize classification outcomes.

6.5 RQ5: Usefulness of Self-assessment

Figure 8 illustrates the potential of leveraging the LLMs' confidence assessments to reduce the human effort required for reviewing invariants classified as *true-positives*. The higher average confidence levels associated with *TP* invariants compared to *FP* invariants indicate some utility in the LLMs' self-assessment of confidence.

However, the determination of an effective cut-off point for categorizing an invariant as *TP* remains ambiguous. A significant overlap exists between the *TP* and *FP* invariants, suggesting that a considerable number of invariants would still necessitate manual verification. Consequently, the reliability of the confidence assessments is not definitively established, and their practical usefulness may be limited or even misleading.

Nevertheless, we believe that the additional information provided in the *Prompt* and the reasoning responses generated by the LLM could prove beneficial for human evaluators. This supplementary context can potentially enhance the evaluators' decision-making process, enabling them to focus their efforts more effectively when reviewing the invariants. But further studies, involving human evaluators are necessary to confirm this.

6.6 Threats to Validity

Several potential threats to the validity of our study should be acknowledged: **Internal Validity:** The performance of LLMs in filtering invariants may be influenced by various uncontrolled factors, such as the inherent biases present in the training data of the models. Additionally, the specific configurations and parameters chosen for the experiments, including the prompt engineering strategies and the settings for different models, could affect the outcomes. Future studies should consider conducting more controlled experiments to isolate these variables. **External Validity:** Our study is based on a specific set of APIs and invariant types, which may limit the generalizability of the results to other contexts. While the APIs used in our experiments are publicly available and cover a range of operations, the findings may not apply to proprietary APIs or those with significantly different specifications. Further research is needed to assess the performance of LLMs in diverse environments and with various invariant categories. **Construct Validity:** In our experiments, we used the LLMs' self-assessed confidence as a measure of classification reliability. We did not use log probabilities (logprobs) for this purpose due to their incompatibility with the function calling feature used in our setup. Further experiments using logprobs could potentially provide a more nuanced understanding of the LLMs' confidence in their classifications.

7 Conclusions and Future Work

In this work, we investigated the effectiveness of Large Language Models (LLMs) in classifying dynamically detected invariants as *true-positives* or *false-positives*. Through a series of experiments, we observed that performance varied significantly based on the level of detail in the instructions and data provided to the LLMs. Additionally, we noted distinct performance differences among the various LLMs utilized in our study. Crucially, our analysis revealed that the type of invariant served as the strongest predictor of classification performance. Overall, our research highlights the potential of LLMs to reduce the manual overhead associated with filtering *false-positives* in invariant detection, thereby improving the efficiency of the detection process.

Although we believe our findings provide useful insights, there remain several avenues for future research to further improve the application of LLMs in this domain. First, evaluating LLM classification performance across a broader range of APIs and invariant types would help validate and generalize our findings. Additionally, investigating the potential benefits of integrating multiple LLMs could leverage their respective strengths, leading to a more robust classification framework. Moreover, exploring alternative methods for assessing model confidence, such as utilizing log probabilities in a different experimental setup, could yield deeper insights into the reliability of classifications. Fine-tuning existing models may also improve classification results. As new models emerge, such as *GPT-o1*, it would be beneficial to evaluate their performance. Lastly, employing LLMs to derive invariants directly from OpenAPI specifications using *Few-shot Prompting* presents an exciting opportunity to enhance the efficiency and accuracy of invariant detection.

Acknowledgement. The research reported in this paper has been funded by BMK, BMAW, and the State of Upper Austria in the frame of the SCCH competence center INTEGRATE (FFG grant no. 892418) part of the FFG COMET Competence Centers for Excellent Technologies Programme.

References

1. Alonso, J.C., Segura, S., Ruiz-Cortés, A.: AGORA: automated generation of test oracles for REST apis. In: Proceedings of the 32nd ACM SIGSOFT International Symposium on Software Testing and Analysis, ISSTA 2023, Seattle, WA, USA, 17-21 July 2023, pp. 1018–1030. ACM (2023). https://doi.org/10.1145/3597926.3598114
2. Blasi, A., et al.: Translating code comments to procedure specifications. In: Proceedings of the 27th ACM SIGSOFT International Symposium on Software Testing and Analysis, ISSTA 2018, Amsterdam, The Netherlands, 16-21 July 2018, pp. 242–253. ACM (2018). https://doi.org/10.1145/3213846.3213872

3. Chuor, P., Ittoo, A., Heng, S.: User story classification with machine learning and llms. In: Knowledge Science, Engineering and Management - 17th International Conference, KSEM 2024, Birmingham, UK, 16-18 August 2024, Proceedings, Part I. LNCS, vol. 14884, pp. 161–175. Springer (2024). https://doi.org/10.1007/978-981-97-5492-2_13
4. Dinella, E., Ryan, G., Mytkowicz, T., Lahiri, S.K.: TOGA: a neural method for test oracle generation. In: 44th IEEE/ACM 44th International Conference on Software Engineering, ICSE 2022, Pittsburgh, PA, USA, 25-27 May 2022, pp. 2130–2141. ACM (2022). https://doi.org/10.1145/3510003.3510141
5. Ernst, M.D., et al.: The daikon system for dynamic detection of likely invariants. Sci. Comput. Program. **69**(1–3), 35–45 (2007). https://doi.org/10.1016/J.SCICO.2007.01.015
6. Gay, G., Rayadurgam, S., Heimdahl, M.P.E.: Improving the accuracy of oracle verdicts through automated model steering. In: ACM/IEEE International Conference on Automated Software Engineering, ASE 2014, Vasteras, Sweden, 15 - 19 September 2014, pp. 527–538. ACM (2014). https://doi.org/10.1145/2642937.2642989
7. Geng, J., Cai, F., Wang, Y., Koeppl, H., Nakov, P., Gurevych, I.: A survey of confidence estimation and calibration in large language models. In: Proceedings of the 2024 Conference of the North American Chapter of the Association for Computational Linguistics: Human Language Technologies (Volume 1: Long Papers), NAACL 2024, Mexico City, Mexico, 16-21 June 2024, pp. 6577–6595 (2024). https://doi.org/10.18653/V1/2024.NAACL-LONG.366
8. Goffi, A., Gorla, A., Ernst, M.D., Pezzè, M.: Automatic generation of oracles for exceptional behaviors. In: Proceedings of the 25th International Symposium on Software Testing and Analysis, ISSTA 2016, Saarbrücken, Germany, 18-20 July 2016, pp. 213–224. ACM (2016). https://doi.org/10.1145/2931037.2931061
9. Hou, X., et al.: Large language models for software engineering: a systematic literature review. ACM Trans. Softw. Eng. Methodol. (2023). https://doi.org/10.1145/3695988
10. Jin, H., Huang, L., Cai, H., Yan, J., Li, B., Chen, H.: From llms to llm-based agents for software engineering: A survey of current, challenges and future. CoRR abs/arxiv: 2408.02479 (2024). https://doi.org/10.48550/ARXIV.2408.02479
11. Kim, M., Stennett, T., Shah, D., Sinha, S., Orso, A.: Leveraging large language models to improve REST API testing. In: Proceedings of the 2024 ACM/IEEE 44th International Conference on Software Engineering: New Ideas and Emerging Results, NIER@ICSE 2024, Lisbon, Portugal, 14-20 April 2024, pp. 37–41. ACM (2024). https://doi.org/10.1145/3639476.3639769
12. Lee, Y., Jeong, S., Kim, J.: Improving LLM classification of logical errors by integrating error relationship into prompts. In: Generative Intelligence and Intelligent Tutoring Systems - 20th International Conference, ITS 2024, Thessaloniki, Greece, 10-13 June 2024, Proceedings, Part I. LNCS, vol. 14798, pp. 91–103. Springer (2024). https://doi.org/10.1007/978-3-031-63028-6_8
13. Molina, F., Ponzio, P., Aguirre, N., Frias, M.F.: Evospex: an evolutionary algorithm for learning postconditions. In: 43rd IEEE/ACM International Conference on Software Engineering, ICSE 2021, Madrid, Spain, 22-30 May 2021, pp. 1223–1235. IEEE (2021). https://doi.org/10.1109/ICSE43902.2021.00112
14. Nie, P., Banerjee, R., Li, J.J., Mooney, R.J., Gligoric, M.: Learning deep semantics for test completion. In: 45th IEEE/ACM International Conference on Software Engineering, ICSE 2023, Melbourne, Australia, 14-20 May 2023, pp. 2111–2123. IEEE (2023). https://doi.org/10.1109/ICSE48619.2023.00178

15. Vito, G.D., Starace, L.L.L., Martino, S.D., Ferrucci, F., Palomba, F.: Large language models in software engineering: A focus on issue report classification and user acceptance test generation. In: Proceedings of the Ital-IA Intelligenza Artificiale - Thematic Workshops co-located with the 4th CINI National Lab AIIS Conference on Artificial Intelligence (Ital-IA 2024), Naples, Italy, May 29-30, 2024. CEUR Workshop Proceedings, vol. 3762, pp. 48–53. CEUR-WS.org (2024). https://ceur-ws.org/Vol-3762/534.pdf
16. Wang, J., Huang, Y., Chen, C., Liu, Z., Wang, S., Wang, Q.: Software testing with large language models: Survey, landscape, and vision. IEEE Trans. Software Eng. **50**(4), 911–936 (2024). https://doi.org/10.1109/TSE.2024.3368208
17. Watson, C., Tufano, M., Moran, K., Bavota, G., Poshyvanyk, D.: On learning meaningful assert statements for unit test cases. In: ICSE 2020: 42nd International Conference on Software Engineering, Seoul, South Korea, 27 June - 19 July, 2020, pp. 1398–1409. ACM (2020). https://doi.org/10.1145/3377811.3380429
18. Xiong, M., et al.: Can llms express their uncertainty? an empirical evaluation of confidence elicitation in llms. In: The Twelfth International Conference on Learning Representations, ICLR 2024, Vienna, Austria, 7-11 May 2024. OpenReview.net (2024). https://openreview.net/forum?id=gjeQKFxFpZ

Advanced Detection of Source Code Clones via an Ensemble of Unsupervised Similarity Measures

Jorge Martinez-Gil(✉)

Software Competence Center Hagenberg GmbH, Softwarepark 32a, 4232 Hagenberg, Austria
jorge.martinez-gil@scch.at

Abstract. The capability of accurately determining code similarity is crucial in many tasks related to software development. For example, it might be essential to identify code duplicates when performing software maintenance. This research introduces a novel ensemble learning approach for code similarity assessment, combining the strengths of multiple unsupervised similarity measures. The key idea is that the strengths of a diverse set of similarity measures can complement each other and mitigate individual weaknesses, leading to improved performance. Preliminary results show that while Transformers-based CodeBERT and its variant GraphCodeBERT are undoubtedly the best option in the presence of abundant training data, in the case of specific small datasets (up to 500 samples), our ensemble achieves similar results, without prejudice to the interpretability of the resulting solution, and with a much lower associated carbon footprint due to training. The source code of this novel approach can be downloaded from https://github.com/jorge-martinez-gil/ensemble-codesim.

Keywords: Ensemble Learning · Similarity Measures · Code Similarity

1 Introduction

Automatically assessing the degree of similarity between source code fragments presents several challenges ranging from syntactic variability or the use of complex algorithmic structures to the employment of diverse abstraction levels across programming languages [21]. While established techniques and tools exist to address this problem, significant limitations must be addressed. For example, the best-performing approaches need vast training data, their insights are practically intelligible to the human operator, and their associated carbon footprint during the training phase does not bring any positive societal outcome [34].

In order to overcome these issues, this research proposes a novel ensemble approach for improved code similarity assessment. The method combines the outputs of multiple similarity measures to produce better similarity scores. This

J. Fischbach et al. (Eds.): SWQD 2025, LNBIP 544, pp. 72–90, 2025.
https://doi.org/10.1007/978-3-031-89277-6_5

approach is based on the principle that the strengths of diverse similarity measures can complement each other and mitigate individual weaknesses, leading to improved systemic performance.

Extensive empirical evaluations on several datasets have demonstrated the effectiveness of our ensemble learning method. Our method outperformed traditional single-model approaches in all cases (both in scenarios with small and large datasets). Furthermore, our method achieved comparable performance to state-of-the-art methods when solving small datasets without reliance on deep learning techniques, making it a solution to consider under circumstances such as the absence of significant amounts of training data, the need for interpretability, and the wish for a reduced carbon footprint when training.

Therefore, our contribution is not only to guide the aggregation of appropriate unsupervised similarity measures for code similarity but also to pave the way for applications such as source clone detection [39] or code plagiarism assessment [35] in realistic scenarios where there is not too much data for training. In this way, the major contributions of this study are:

- We build upon previous work [32] to curate a comprehensive collection of unsupervised similarity measures to compare the likeness of different code fragments. This collection facilitates a systematic exploration of the most effective measures for assessing source code similarity at low computational cost.
- Furthermore, we investigate the learning of ensembles through bagging and boosting techniques. We aim to develop models with improved code similarity assessment capabilities using the above-mentioned similarity measures.
- We evaluate the proposed ensembles and focus on metrics such as precision, recall, and f-measure. Our findings show that ensembles outperform individual similarity measures and have the potential to rival even the most sophisticated state-of-the-art techniques in the absence of significant training data.

The remainder of this paper is structured as follows: Sect. 2 provides the background on the code similarity assessment challenge and establishes its importance in the software development field. Section 3 explains the unsupervised similarity measures to address this challenge and how we can rely on them to build ensembles with superior performance. Section 4 empirically evaluates the ensembles introduced before using popular benchmark datasets. Section 5 offers a detailed analysis and discussion of the experimental results. Finally, the paper concludes with lessons learned and outlines future lines of work.

2 State-of-the-Art

The existence of many programming languages and individual coding styles poses a challenge for determining the degree of likeness between source code fragments [3]. Despite that, unsupervised similarity measures demonstrate reasonable adaptability when working with code written in multiple languages or according to various styles, so it can be accepted that they are good indicators of code similarity [32]. This feature is also important in many scenarios, such as maintenance, whereby increased complexity is commonplace [18].

Code similarity has gained significant attention, mainly due to its application in clone detection, an active area of research [1,2,15,27,50]. Language model-based strategies are often noted for their superior performance [22]. However, our hypothesis is that unsupervised methods for code similarity evaluation offer several advantages for addressing aspects that should not be overlooked:

- Capturing the meaning of code is a complex task, as functionally equivalent code fragments may exhibit superficial differences or, on the contrary, share surface-level similarities while having entirely different purposes. Some unsupervised techniques specifically focus on the semantic intent rather than syntactic details.
- Since unsupervised techniques eliminate the need for labeled training data, they reduce the overhead of establishing a ground truth. While labeled examples remain valuable for validating the effectiveness of these methods, these examples are not a prerequisite for deployment.
- Codebases often contain comments and other non-functional elements embedded within the core logic. Specific unsupervised methods can distinguish between meaningful code patterns and just incidental material.
- Unsupervised methods can accommodate the diversity of programming languages and coding styles. This mitigates the need for a complex strategy that attempts to account for all possible variations.

We acknowledge the superior capabilities of language models when confronted with this challenge. However, we also recognize and aim to demonstrate that alternative models, which excel in specific areas, could be employed under certain conditions across a wide range of scenarios. For instance, these models may be more suitable in situations where only limited datasets are available or where the logic of the proposed solution needs to be clearly understood.

2.1 Unsupervised Code Similarity

There are various techniques to assess the similarity between source code fragments, each with its unique perspective based on certain features of the code fragments being compared. The following is a list that we have already proposed previously [32], consisting of twenty-one distinct unsupervised approaches. Table 1 presents all these similarity measures.

According to existing research [32], it is unrealistic to think that these techniques alone can deliver performance equivalent to the state-of-the-art. However, we aim to show how their aggregation can do so under certain conditions.

2.2 Supervised Code Similarity

Supervised code similarity is a well-studied field and has yielded the best results to date [42–44,47,49]. Although among the existing approaches, CodeBERT [12]

Table 1. Comparison of Different Unsupervised Similarity Approaches

Approach	Description	Ref.
Abstract Syntax Trees (ASTs) Similarity	Examines the hierarchical structures of code to identify structural similarities between different ASTs.	[26]
Bag-of-Words Similarity	Counts the occurrence of words in texts, comparing these frequencies while ignoring word order and structural context.	[9]
Code Embeddings Similarity	Uses vector representations of code for comparison, evaluating similarity based on these embeddings. This technique is used without recalibration (zero-shot) here.	[4]
Comments Similarity	Focuses on comparing code comments to facilitate documentation and understanding, using traditional text similarity methods.	[33]
Fuzzy Matching Similarity	Adapts string comparison techniques for minor syntactical variations to code similarity assessment.	[41]
Function Calls Similarity	Compares source code fragments based on their function names.	[46]
Graph-based Similarity	Relies on the relationships in graphs, representing data structures or code dependencies, to determine similarity.	[48]
Jaccard Similarity	Uses set intersection and union to evaluate similarity in text analysis and information retrieval contexts.	[16]
Levenshtein Similarity	Measures the minimum number of edits needed to transform one string into another, reflecting similarity.	[29]
Longest Common Subsequence (LCS) Similarity	Identifies the longest sequence of items that two series share, indicating similarity.	[7]
Metrics Similarity	Involves computing various code-related metrics and comparing these values to estimate similarity.	[36]
N-grams Similarity	Compares texts based on the occurrence of contiguous sequences of n items, evaluating shared n-grams.	[10]
Output Analysis Similarity	Assesses the similarity of program outputs by applying traditional text similarity metrics.	[33]

(*continued*)

Table 1. (*continued*)

Approach	Description	Ref.
Perceptual Hashing Similarity	Adapts techniques from image similarity, using hash codes from visual representations of code to measure similarity.	[37]
Program Dependence Graph Similarity	Assesses the similarity between codes by analyzing their program dependence graphs, representing the dependencies between their elements.	[28]
Rolling Hash Similarity	Employs a dynamically updating hash to compare substrings in large texts, adapted for code comparison.	[17]
RKR-GST Similarity	Targets code similarity detection by identifying maximal sequences of contiguous matching tokens in texts.	[45]
Semdiff Similarity	Detects semantic differences between program versions, evaluating the impact of code changes on semantics.	[19]
Semantic Clone Similarity	Assesses code fragment similarity based on the semantic meanings of program element names.	[13]
TF-IDF Similarity	Common in text analysis, compares texts based on the relative importance of terms, using weighted term frequencies.	[23]
Winnow Similarity	Identifies similar texts by hashing and comparing text fingerprints.	[40]

and its variant GraphCodeBERT [14] stand out. CodeBERT is a variant of BERT [11], and empirical results show that it is the leading technology to understand source code expressed in different general-purpose programming languages. It excels at tasks like generating documentation, creating code, and comparing similar pieces of code. The idea behind CodeBERT is to combine techniques from language processing with an understanding of code and training on a wide range of programming languages and their associated comments. Results show CodeBERT is very good at detecting similarities between source code fragments, as demonstrated by its performance in the resolution of benchmark datasets for clone detection [12]. However, an additional fine-tuning phase on the pre-trained model over the actual data is usually required to obtain optimal results. This fine-tuning process helps the model adapt to the specific characteristics of the dataset, further improving its ability to identify subtle patterns and relationships within the code.

2.3 Contribution over the State-of-the-Art

This research introduces a novel ensemble learning approach for code similarity assessment. The rationale behind combining multiple unsupervised similarity measures is to benefit from the strengths of individual approaches while mitigating their weaknesses. This strategy is helpful in scenarios where deep learning is not optimal due to the absence of significant training data, when prioritizing model interpretability without significantly compromising performance, or even when seeking to minimize the environmental impact.

Our work's focus is eminently practical. In fact, we evaluate our ensembles on benchmark datasets to confirm the approach's superiority over traditional techniques. Furthermore, we offer our code as open-source since this availability might promote transparency and collaborative advancement.

3 Ensemble Approach

We propose using an ensemble of unsupervised similarity measures to improve the performance when assessing code similarity. The rationale behind combining several unsupervised similarity measures is to offer a more accurate evaluation than strategies using just one measure [31]. Therefore, we first define the problem, introduce the concept of an ensemble, and discuss bagging and boosting as the two most prominent techniques for building ensembles. These techniques for building ensembles help aggregate different unsupervised similarity measures, leading usually to an improved strategy.

3.1 Problem Statement

We can define code similarity as follows: Given a set of code fragments $S = \{C_1, C_2, \ldots, C_n\}$, we aim to find a function $f : S \times S \rightarrow [0, 1]$ that measures the similarity between any two fragments C_i and C_j.

The function f should map a pair (C_i, C_j) to a continuous value within the real interval $[0, 1]$:

1. $f(C_i, C_j) = 0$ indicates absolute code dissimilarity.
2. $f(C_i, C_j) = 1$ indicates equivalent code.
3. The value of $f(C_i, C_j)$ increases with increasing similarity between C_i and C_j.

Some applications can be built from this definition [38]. For example, code clone detection can be performed by applying a threshold value to differentiate between clones and non-clones [25].

$$\text{Clone}(C_i, C_j) = \begin{cases} \text{True}, & \text{if } f(C_i, C_j) > \theta \\ \text{False}, & \text{otherwise} \end{cases}$$

In addition, something similar can also be done to determine whether or not the code was plagiarized in an academic environment [5], for example. These two challenges of a very similar nature will be studied in more detail later in the paper.

3.2 Ensemble Definition

Let $S = \{s_1, s_2, \ldots, s_n\}$ be a set of code fragments and $M = \{m_1, m_2, \ldots, m_{21}\}$ be a set of unsupervised similarity measures. An ensemble E aims to aggregate similarity measures such as:

$$E(s_a, s_b) = \alpha_1 \cdot m_1(s_a, s_b) + \ldots + \alpha_{21} \cdot m_{21}(s_a, s_b)$$

where α_i represents the weight of each similarity measure, and $\sum_{i=1}^{21} \alpha_i = 1$.

Each $m_i(s_a, s_b)$ returns a similarity score in the real range [0, 1], where 0 indicates no similarity, and 1 indicates equivalent code fragments. The ensemble E, therefore, also returns a score in the real range [0, 1], effectively aggregating the individual similarity assessments into a measure.

There are several techniques for learning ensembles, almost all based on a purely data-driven strategy. In the context of this work, and for practical reasons, we focus on two: bagging and boosting. Other techniques, such as stacking, will not be considered here because they have already been addressed in similar problems in the past, such as [30]. Although an in-depth study of each of these techniques is beyond the scope of this study, we offer below a brief description of how these ensemble-building strategies operate.

3.3 Bagging

The idea behind bagging is to train multiple instances of the same model with different data subsets and aggregate their predictions [8].

Formally, let D denote the original dataset and M the number of subsets to create. The subsets D_i for $i \in \{1, 2, \ldots, M\}$ are generated through random sampling with replacement. For each subset D_i, a model f_i is trained. Given an unsupervised similarity measure S, we compute the similarity score for each subset:

$$S_i = S(f_i, D_i) \quad \text{for } i \in \{1, 2, \ldots, M\}.$$

The final aggregated prediction is obtained by averaging the individual predictions from all models:

$$\hat{y} = \frac{1}{M} \sum_{i=1}^{M} f_i(D).$$

This technique helps reduce variance and improve the stability of the model.

3.4 Boosting

The idea behind boosting is to train multiple models, with each model instance focusing on the errors of the previous one [6].

Formally, let D denote the dataset and N the number of boosting rounds. We start with an initial model f_1 and iterate sequentially through each round. For each round $t \in \{1, 2, \ldots, N\}$, we train a model f_t with a focus on the errors made by the previous models. Let S denote a set of unsupervised similarity measures.

At each round, we update a weight distribution w_t over the dataset based on the errors of f_t, aiming to emphasize the misclassified cases. The similarity scores for the current model f_t are calculated as:

$$S_t = S(f_t, D) \quad \text{for } t \in \{1, 2, \ldots, N\}.$$

The final aggregated prediction is obtained by combining the models using their respective weights:

$$\hat{y} = \sum_{t=1}^{N} \alpha_t f_t(D),$$

where α_t is the weight assigned to each model f_t based on its performance in reducing the error. This sequential training allows for iterative refinement of the predictions.

3.5 Differences with the Transformer Architecture

Using an ensemble of unsupervised semantic similarity measures for code similarity assessment offers several advantages over relying solely on a model like CodeBERT [11], or its more powerful variant GraphCodeBERT [14]. The ensemble approach combines different unsupervised similarity measures, each capturing unique aspects of code, thus providing a diverse analysis that can reduce individual biases and improve performance.

Ensembles are also more flexible and do not require massive labeled data, making them suitable for diverse programming languages and code domains. Therefore, our approach benefits from the strengths of multiple unsupervised similarity measures, potentially outperforming all of them. Transformers-inspired solutions can face challenges with interpretability due to their complex attention mechanisms and might struggle with out-of-distribution or noisy code fragments. However, if sufficient data is available and there are no requirements beyond performance, results from transformer architectures should be much superior.

4 Empirical Evaluation

In previous work [32], we show that unsupervised similarity measures exhibit strengths in different domains. Some excel in textual comparisons, making them ideal for identifying cloned text. Others prioritize the detection of functional similarity, while specific measures specialize in uncovering structural resemblances between code and textual elements. The optimal choice of measure ultimately depends on the composition of the benchmark dataset. However, it is not reasonable to ask a human expert to do that since it would require many hours of work, and the result would be prone to errors since the task is far from trivial.

The good news is that bagging and boosting algorithms, with their data-driven strategies, will decide the inclusion and importance of each of the simple unsupervised similarity measures.

4.1 Baseline

In this study, we compare our ensembles using two strategies. First, a weak baseline consists of obtaining better results than each similarity measure considered individually. Secondly, a strong baseline consists of the state-of-the-art conformed by CodeBERT [11] and its variant GraphCodeBERT [14].

In this regard, state-of-the-art models start with an initial phase where a dataset of code fragments is loaded and randomly split into training, validation, and test sets. The primary process focuses on training the model to recognize clone pairs, with a trainer set up according to parameters like epoch count, batch size, and learning rate. Model effectiveness is assessed by averaging performance metrics over multiple executions; our study includes up to 10 independent runs for a thorough evaluation.

4.2 Small-Scale Dataset

Firstly, we use the IR-Plag dataset [24]. This dataset was designed for benchmarking code similarity techniques. It contains code files deliberately crafted to simulate patterns of academic plagiarism. Although primarily intended for plagiarism detection, its characteristics align with our goals due to the overlap between plagiarized and cloned code, which involves replication (though the intent may differ). The IR-Plag dataset encompasses a variety of complexities without strictly classifying the clone types.

The dataset consists of seven original code files. A substantial portion, 355 files (77%), are labeled as plagiarized, indicating a high prevalence of duplication. One hundred five files are considered non-plagiarized, potentially representing modified or derivative works. This yields a total of 467 code files. Collectively, these files contain 59,201 tokens, with 540 unique tokens underlining the dataset's lexical diversity. File sizes exhibit variation, ranging from 286 tokens (largest) to 40 tokens (smallest), with an average file size of approximately 126 tokens. Therefore, although small in size, it is a dataset with a high compositional diversity of programming elements.

4.3 Large-Scale Dataset

Secondly, we use the BigCloneBench dataset, a benchmark collection created to evaluate how well different code clone detection strategies perform. It helps tackle the challenge of finding duplicate code. It includes a variety of programming languages, and its data comes from actual software and student projects. This mix makes it an interesting resource for evaluating clone detection in real-life situations. This dataset is usually used in training solutions to make code more maintainable.

The dataset is divided into three subsets: training, validation, and testing. The training set contains 901,028 items, while the validation and testing sets contain 415,416 items each. This distribution is outlined to ensure proper training, validation, and testing of the model. This setup allows for consistent evaluation of various approaches, enabling a fair comparison of their effectiveness in identifying code clones under the same conditions.

4.4 Evaluation Criteria

In principle, measuring the accuracy of the different techniques is appropriate. That is the percentage of occasions in which the strategy under study succeeded or failed in predicting the similarity of code fragments. However, this metric is strongly discouraged for unbalanced datasets because the mere fact of constantly repeating the label of the most numerous classes in the test set will yield a high value that may be misleading.

Therefore, the community prefers other metrics to assess the fitness of a clone detection strategy. For instance, the Precision/Recall evaluation method is popular because it emphasizes the importance of positive classes by separately assessing false positives (precision) and false negatives (recall). It penalizes the model for not identifying positive cases and for incorrect positive predictions. Subsequently, one can compute a harmonic mean of these two metrics, known as the F-measure, which serves as a basis for a homogeneous ranking.

4.5 Hardware Requirements

Please note that all the computations of the unsupervised similarity measures and the learning of their ensembles have been done on a CPU 11th Gen Intel(R) Core(TM) i7-1185G7 a 3.00 GHz with 32 GB for RAM (TDP of 50 W approx.), while the configuration and execution of the baselines with CodeBERT and GraphCodeBERT has required a GPU Tesla V100-PCIE-16 GB (TDP of 300 W approx). This difference in hardware requirements shows the practicality of our ensemble approach, offering a solution that operates effectively without relying on high-end GPUs.

4.6 Results

Table 2 shows us the results obtained for the first benchmark dataset, i.e., the small-scale IR-Plag. It can be seen that some unsupervised similarity measures are pretty good on their own if one looks at the f-measure. However, it is striking that ensembles obtain the best results, so we far exceed our weak baseline. Please note that we do not study time consumption issues here as they have been studied previously [32].

Table 3 establishes a comparative for the state-of-the-art published to this dataset. On the one hand, it can be seen that the ensembles can perform better than CodeBERT. The reason is that they perform better without large data for

Table 2. Summary of the results obtained for the IR-Plag dataset

Approach	Precision	Recall	F-Measure
Abstract Syntax Tree	0.95	0.30	0.45
Bag-of-Words	0.93	0.19	0.31
CodeBERT	0.91	0.03	0.05
Comment Sim.	0.88	0.40	0.55
Output Analysis	0.88	0.93	0.90
Function Calls	0.85	0.67	0.75
Fuzzy Matching	0.82	0.50	0.62
Graph Matching	0.82	0.91	0.86
Rolling Hash	0.94	0.20	0.33
Perceptual Hash	0.89	0.41	0.57
Jaccard	0.99	0.26	0.42
Longest Common Subsequence	0.78	0.97	0.87
Levenshtein	0.82	0.76	0.79
Metrics comparison	0.81	0.57	0.67
N-Grams	0.84	0.83	0.84
Program Dependence Graph	0.85	0.39	0.53
Rabin-Karp	0.87	0.47	0.61
Semantic Clone	0.94	0.24	0.38
Semdiff method	0.87	0.25	0.39
TDF-IDF	0.97	0.17	0.29
Winnow	0.89	0.65	0.75
Boosting	0.88	0.99	0.93
Bagging	0.95	0.97	0.96

training. This is even though several combinations of different partitions have been evaluated: 60-20-20, 70-15-15, and 80-10-10 on training, validation, and test, respectively. We are reporting here the best average obtained. GraphCodeBERT matches our best results, but given the disadvantages discussed in this study, our solution may be more appropriate when working with small datasets, when interpretability is required, or when minimizing environmental impact is a priority.

Table 4 shows us the results of the different unsupervised similarity measures over the BigCloneBench dataset. These results estimate over 25,000 samples (6% of the dataset) because we do not have enough computational power to analyze the complete dataset. We also discard similarity calculations in scenarios requiring more than 20 s of computation; otherwise, the process may require many days. Furthermore, similarity by output analysis cannot be performed in this context due to the high computational requirements of packaging, compiling, executing, and comparing several million code samples.

Table 3. State-of-the-art for the IR-Plag dataset. Due to the small size of the dataset, several datasets partitions have been tested for the CodeBERT and GraphCodeBERT fine-tuning process

Approach	Precision	Recall	F-Measure
CodeBERT	0.72	1.00	0.84
Output Analysis	0.88	0.93	0.90
Boosting	0.88	0.99	0.93
GraphCodeBERT	0.98	0.95	0.96
Bagging	0.95	0.97	0.96

Table 4. Summary of the results obtained for the BigCloneBench dataset

Approach	Precision	Recall	F-Measure
Abstract Syntax Tree	0.15	0.47	0.23
Bag-of-Words	0.27	0.62	0.38
CodeBERT	0.18	0.29	0.23
Comment Sim.	0.20	0.31	0.25
Output Analysis	0.00	0.00	0.00
Function Calls	0.40	0.62	0.48
Fuzzy Matching	0.38	0.43	0.40
Graph Matching	0.16	0.46	0.23
Rolling Hash	0.21	0.23	0.22
Perceptual Hash	0.15	0.78	0.24
Jaccard	0.27	0.62	0.38
Longest Common Subsequence	0.22	0.47	0.30
Levenshtein	0.33	0.23	0.27
Metrics comparison	0.15	0.72	0.25
N-Grams	0.32	0.45	0.37
Program Dependence Graph	0.18	0.44	0.26
Rabin-Karp	0.15	0.22	0.18
Semantic Clone	0.23	0.43	0.30
Semdiff method	0.18	0.26	0.22
TDF-IDF	0.27	0.63	0.38
Winnow	0.20	0.71	0.31
Bagging	0.85	0.42	0.56
Boosting	0.79	0.45	0.57

Our solution can be used on the total set, and sufficient computational power is available if desired. Future work can address this limitation by improving computational efficiency or utilizing higher-performance hardware to handle larger datasets more effectively.

As can be seen, each technique individually performs far below what would be required in a real environment. Therefore, there are better candidates for integration into real-world systems. However, their systematic aggregation through bagging or boosting techniques yields superior results, so we far exceeded our weak baseline. This shows that while individual techniques are insufficient for practical use, combining them improves performance, making the results much more applicable to real-world scenarios.

Table 5 establishes a comparative for the state-of-the-art published to this dataset. For the fine-tuning of CodeBERT and GraphCodeBERT, we rely on the configuration outlined by the authors of the original papers. At the same time, the numbers relative to our strategies are estimated. The reason is that the bagging and boosting strategies have been tested using the seven most promising unsupervised similarity measures from the 415,416 samples of the test partition. These promising measures have been obtained from a preliminary study; please refer to the source code for more information. The reason is, again, not having enough computational resources to operate over the whole search space.

Table 5. State-of-the-art for the BigCloneBench dataset

Approach	Precision	Recall	F-Measure
Deckard [20]	0.93	0.02	0.03
RtvNN [44]	0.95	0.01	0.01
Bagging	0.85	0.42	0.56
Boosting	0.79	0.45	0.57
CDLH [43]	0.92	0.74	0.82
ASTNN [49]	0.92	0.94	0.93
CodeBERT [12]	0.95	0.93	0.94
FA-AST-GMN [42]	0.96	0.94	0.95
TBBCD [47]	0.94	0.96	0.95
GraphCodeBERT [14]	0.95	0.95	0.95

It is possible to see that, although computational constraints limit the results for bagging and boosting, they still demonstrate notable performance compared to several other methods. Expanding the evaluation to cover the entire search space could provide a more accurate comparison and further insights into the potential of these strategies.

5 Discussion

Our experiments demonstrate the effectiveness of ensemble learning for assessing code similarity. Although the results are questionable when the training data are abundant, an equivalent performance is observed when working with small datasets. Our study shows that a small dataset in this context is less than 500 samples.

In any case, integrating diverse unsupervised similarity measures seems effective since our approach surpasses the performance of single-measure strategies regarding code clone detection. Our ensemble approach mitigates the inherent limitations of individual similarity measures. Aggregating results from multiple measures compensate for the shortcomings of any single similarity measure. For instance, a structure-focused measure may overlook semantically equivalent code with superficial syntactic differences.

Furthermore, the adaptable nature of our ensemble approach offers other significant benefits. We can incorporate a variety of similarity measures, enabling us to tailor the strategy for specific applications. If plagiarism detection is the primary objective, structure-focused measures could be given a higher weight, or semantic-oriented measures might be prioritized for code reuse identification, among others.

Moreover, future work could explore the dynamic weighting of similarity measures based on the task's specific requirements, further enhancing the proposed approach's adaptability. In general, our research yielded some lessons learned, detailed below.

5.1 Lessons Learned

Our experiments show that some unsupervised code similarity methods work reasonably well for finding source code clones. Therefore, it could make sense to integrate these methods to help improve software development under certain circumstances. For example,

1. Our ensembles can find duplicate code to rewrite as reusable parts at a low cost. This is important since code reuse is vital to many software-related tasks. For example, developers can save time, reduce redundancy, and improve maintainability, which are essential for efficient and sustainable software development practices.
2. Real-world code can be unstructured, but our ensembles of unsupervised methods can manage this noise and variation, which is particularly relevant in scenarios with little labeled data. This ability to work effectively without requiring extensive labeled datasets makes this strategy suitable for applications in resource-constrained environments.
3. A human operator cannot easily interpret the Transformers-like architectures on which CodeBERT is based. Moreover, they have a huge carbon footprint when trained [34]. Our approach may be reasonable in situations where these two aspects are critical.
4. The simplicity of our unsupervised methods makes them more accessible to developers without extensive expertise in machine learning. This reduces the barriers to adoption and enables wider use in practical scenarios where simplicity and efficiency are valued over cutting-edge accuracy.

However, there are areas where the performance of our ensembles could be improved, particularly in benefiting from large training datasets, optimizing computational efficiency for extensive codebases, and tailoring the approach to specific software engineering tasks. These aspects are discussed below.

5.2 Limitations

Our proposed approach has yielded promising results; however, some aspects still need improvement. First, when dealing with abundant training data, the performance of our ensembles falls substantially below the benchmarks set by state-of-the-art models. Addressing this weakness would require enhancing our ensemble strategy to integrate advanced pre-trained embeddings, for example. However, this would be to the detriment of one of our greatest strengths: the possibility of interpreting the resulting model.

Second, scalability presents a challenge; as codebases expand in size and complexity, the computational burden of implementing multiple similarity measures increases considerably. This escalation demands the integration of more efficient optimization techniques to manage and mitigate the increased processing requirements. Possible strategies include employing approximate methods for similarity computation, implementing parallel processing, or incorporating some hardware acceleration to reduce execution time.

Lastly, while our ensemble method offers theoretical interpretability, its practical use demands a more pragmatic approach. This might include developing intuitive visualizations or explanations that clarify how different similarity measures contribute to the final prediction. Such approaches could improve user trust and adoption by providing more precise insights into why specific code fragments are deemed similar. It seems reasonable to think that further work is crucial to demonstrate how the model identifies similar code fragments, improving transparency and usability in practice.

6 Conclusions and Future Work

Evaluating code similarity is a crucial component of many software development tasks. In this study, we have explored unsupervised similarity measures, leveraging their independence from labeled data and adaptability to diverse coding styles. Our findings show the efficacy of ensemble learning approaches in code similarity assessment. We have developed a strategy that surpasses traditional techniques by aggregating multiple measures, achieving performance comparable to state-of-the-art standards without significant training data.

As code becomes more complex, there is a growing need for accurate and efficient ways to measure code similarity. The software industry's ever-changing nature shows us the vital role that unsupervised similarity measures could play in this context. While supervised approaches are superior in performance, unsupervised techniques often offer advantages of another kind.

Future work could further explore the potential of unsupervised code similarity methods. Future research could also evaluate the efficacy of other ensemble techniques and examine the applicability of transfer learning for improved performance. The ultimate goal is to advance code analysis automation. This development could significantly reduce the need for manual intervention across all phases of the software development process, thereby increasing efficiency and productivity in the field. Additionally, incorporating these methods into development environments could provide real-time assistance to programmers, helping to detect and address potential issues more efficiently during the software development process.

Acknowledgments. The author thanks all the anonymous reviewers for their invaluable help in improving the manuscript. This research has been funded by the Federal Ministry for Climate Action, Environment, Energy, Mobility, Innovation, and Technology (BMK), the Federal Ministry for Digital and Economic Affairs (BMDW), and the State of Upper Austria in the frame of SCCH, a center in the COMET - Competence Centers for Excellent Technologies Programme managed by Austrian Research Promotion Agency FFG.

Data Availability and Access. The data and the source code to reproduce this research are available at: https://github.com/jorge-martinez-gil/ensemble-codesim. The manuscript is also available as a preprint at https://arxiv.org/abs/2405.02095. At least a Tesla V100 GPU or a more advanced device is recommended for optimal performance, at least for the configuration and execution of the baselines with CodeBERT and GraphCodeBERT.

References

1. Abdelkader, M.: A novel method for code clone detection based on minimally random kernel convolutional transform. IEEE Access **12**, 158579–158596 (2024)
2. Abid, S., Cai, X., Jiang, L.: Measuring model alignment for code clone detection using causal interpretation. Empir. Softw. Eng. **30**(2), 46 (2025)
3. Ain, Q.U., Butt, W.H., Anwar, M.W., Azam, F., Maqbool, B.: A systematic review on code clone detection. IEEE Access **7**, 86121–86144 (2019)
4. Alon, U., Zilberstein, M., Levy, O., Yahav, E.: code2vec: learning distributed representations of code. Proc. ACM Program. Lang. **3**(POPL), 1–29 (2019)
5. Aniceto, R.C., Holanda, M., Castanho, C., Da Silva, D.: Source code plagiarism detection in an educational context: a literature mapping. In: 2021 IEEE Frontiers in Education Conference (FIE), pp, 1–9. IEEE (2021)
6. Bentéjac, C., Csörgő, A., Martínez-Muñoz, G.: A comparative analysis of gradient boosting algorithms. Artif. Intell. Rev. **54**, 1937–1967 (2021)
7. Bergroth, L., Hakonen, H., Raita, T.: A survey of longest common subsequence algorithms. In: Proceedings Seventh International Symposium on String Processing and Information Retrieval. SPIRE 2000, pp. 39–48. IEEE (2000)
8. Breiman, L.: Bagging predictors. Mach. Learn. **24**, 123–140 (1996)
9. Corley, C.D., Mihalcea, R.: Measuring the semantic similarity of texts. In: Proceedings of the ACL Workshop on Empirical Modeling of Semantic Equivalence and Entailment, pp. 13–18 (2005)

10. Damashek, M.: Gauging similarity with n-grams: language-independent categorization of text. Science **267**(5199), 843–848 (1995)
11. Devlin, J., Chang, M.W., Lee, K., Toutanova, K.: BERT: pre-training of deep bidirectional transformers for language understanding. In: Burstein, J., Doran, C., Solorio, T. (eds.) Proceedings of the 2019 Conference of the North American Chapter of the Association for Computational Linguistics: Human Language Technologies, NAACL-HLT 2019, Minneapolis, MN, USA, 2-7 June 2019, Volume 1 (Long and Short Papers), pp. 4171–4186. Association for Computational Linguistics (2019)
12. Feng, Z., et al.: CodeBERT: a pre-trained model for programming and natural languages. In: Cohn, T., He, Y., Liu, Y. (eds.) Findings of the Association for Computational Linguistics: EMNLP 2020, Online Event, 16-20 November 2020, volume EMNLP 2020 of Findings of ACL, pp. 1536–1547. Association for Computational Linguistics (2020)
13. Gabel, M., Jiang, L., Su, Z.: Scalable detection of semantic clones. In: Proceedings of the 30th International Conference on Software Engineering, pp. 321–330 (2008)
14. Guo, D., et al. GraphCodeBERT: pre-training code representations with data flow. arXiv preprint arXiv:2009.08366 (2020)
15. Gupta, A., Goyal, R.: A generative AI-driven method-level semantic clone detection based on the structural and semantical comparison of methods. IEEE Access **12**, 70773–70791 (2024)
16. Haque, S., Eberhart, Z., Bansal, A., McMillan, C.: Semantic similarity metrics for evaluating source code summarization. In: Proceedings of the 30th IEEE/ACM International Conference on Program Comprehension, pp. 36–47 (2022)
17. Hartanto, A.D., Syaputra, A., Pristyanto, Y.: Best parameter selection of Rabin-Karp algorithm in detecting document similarity. In: 2019 International Conference on Information and Communications Technology (ICOIACT), pp. 457–461. IEEE (2019)
18. Higo, Y., Ueda, Y., Kamiya, T., Kusumoto, S., Inoue, K.: On software maintenance process improvement based on code clone analysis. In: Oivo, M., Komi-Sirviö, S. (eds.) PROFES 2002. LNCS, vol. 2559, pp. 185–197. Springer, Heidelberg (2002). https://doi.org/10.1007/3-540-36209-6_17
19. Horwitz, S.: Identifying the semantic and textual differences between two versions of a program. In: Proceedings of the ACM SIGPLAN 1990 Conference on Programming Language Design and Implementation, pp. 234–245 (1990)
20. Jiang, L., Misherghi, G., Su, Z., Glondu, S.: Deckard: scalable and accurate tree-based detection of code clones. In: 29th International Conference on Software Engineering (ICSE 2007), pp. 96–105. IEEE (2007)
21. Juergens, E., Deissenboeck, F., Hummel, B., Wagner, S.: Do code clones matter? In: 2009 IEEE 31st International Conference on Software Engineering, pp. 485–495. IEEE (2009)
22. Karmakar, A., Robbes, R.: What do pre-trained code models know about code? In 2021 36th IEEE/ACM International Conference on Automated Software Engineering (ASE), pp. 1332–1336. IEEE (2021)
23. Karnalim, O.: TF-IDF inspired detection for cross-language source code plagiarism and collusion. Comput. Sci. **21**, 113–136 (2020)
24. Karnalim, O., Budi, S., Toba, H., Joy, M.: Source code plagiarism detection in academia with information retrieval: dataset and the observation. Inf. Educ. **18**(2), 321–344 (2019)
25. Karnalim, O., et al.: Explanation in code similarity investigation. IEEE Access **9**, 59935–59948 (2021)

26. Karnalim, O., Simon: Syntax trees and information retrieval to improve code similarity detection. In: Proceedings of the Twenty-Second Australasian Computing Education Conference, pp. 48–55 (2020)
27. Khajezade, M., Fard, F.H., Shehata, M.S.: Evaluating few-shot and contrastive learning methods for code clone detection. Empir. Softw. Eng. **29**(6), 163 (2024)
28. Krinke, J.: Identifying similar code with program dependence graphs. In: Proceedings Eighth Working Conference on Reverse Engineering, pp. 301–309. IEEE (2001)
29. Levenshtein V.I.: Binary codes capable of correcting deletions, insertions, and reversals. Soviet Phys. Doklady **10**, 707–710 (1966)
30. Martinez-Gil, J.: A comprehensive review of stacking methods for semantic similarity measurement. Mach. Learn. Appl. **10**, 100423 (2022)
31. Martinez-Gil, J.: A comparative study of ensemble techniques based on genetic programming: a case study in semantic similarity assessment. Int. J. Softw. Eng. Knowl. Eng. **33**(2), 289–312 (2023)
32. Martinez-Gil, J.: Source code clone detection using unsupervised similarity measures. In: Bludau, P., Ramler, R., Winkler, D., Bergsmann, J. (eds.) Software Quality as a Foundation for Security - 16th International Conference on Software Quality, SWQD 2024, Vienna, Austria, 23-25 April 2024, Proceedings. LNBIP, vol. 505, pp. 21–37. Springer, Cham (2024). https://doi.org/10.1007/978-3-031-56281-5_2
33. Jorge Martinez-Gil and Jose Manuel Chaves-Gonzalez: A novel method based on symbolic regression for interpretable semantic similarity measurement. Expert Syst. Appl. **160**, 113663 (2020)
34. Martinez-Gil, J., Chaves-Gonzalez, J.M.: Sustainable semantic similarity assessment. J. Intell. Fuzzy Syst. **43**(5), 6163–6174 (2022)
35. Novak, M., Joy, M., Kermek, D.: Source-code similarity detection and detection tools used in academia: a systematic review. ACM Trans. Comput. Educ. (TOCE) **19**(3), 1–37 (2019)
36. Nuñez-Varela, A.S., Pérez-Gonzalez, H.G., Martínez-Perez, F.E., Soubervielle-Montalvo, C.: Source code metrics: a systematic mapping study. J. Syst. Softw. **128**, 164–197 (2017)
37. Ragkhitwetsagul, C., Krinke, J., Marnette, B.: A picture is worth a thousand words: code clone detection based on image similarity. In: 12th IEEE International Workshop on Software Clones, IWSC 2018, Campobasso, Italy, 20 March 2018, pp. 44–50. IEEE Computer Society (2018)
38. Roy, C.K., Cordy, J.R., Koschke, R.: Comparison and evaluation of code clone detection techniques and tools: a qualitative approach. Sci. Comput. Program. **74**(7), 470–495 (2009)
39. Saini, N., Singh, S., et al.: Code clones: detection and management. Procedia Comput. Sci. **132**, 718–727 (2018)
40. Schleimer, S., Wilkerson, D.S., Aiken, A.: Winnowing: local algorithms for document fingerprinting. In: Proceedings of the 2003 ACM SIGMOD International Conference on Management of Data, pp. 76–85 (2003)
41. Singla, N., Garg, D.: String matching algorithms and their applicability in various applications. Int. J. Soft Comput. Eng. **1**(6), 218–222 (2012)
42. Wang, W., Li, G., Ma, B., Xia, X., Jin, Z.: Detecting code clones with graph neural network and flow-augmented abstract syntax tree. In: 2020 IEEE 27th International Conference on Software Analysis, Evolution and Reengineering (SANER), pp. 261–271. IEEE (2020)

43. Wei, H., Li, M., Supervised deep features for software functional clone detection by exploiting lexical and syntactical information in source code. In: IJCAI, pp. 3034–3040 (2017)
44. White, M., Tufano, M., Vendome, C., Poshyvanyk, D.: Deep learning code fragments for code clone detection. In: Proceedings of the 31st IEEE/ACM International Conference on Automated Software Engineering, pp. 87–98 (2016)
45. Wise M.J.: String similarity via greedy string tiling and running Karp-Rabin matching. Online Preprint, Dec **119**(1), 1–17 (1993)
46. Xu, M., et al.: A similarity metric method of obfuscated malware using function-call graph. J. Comput. Virol. Hacking Tech. **9**(1), 35–47 (2013). https://doi.org/10.1007/s11416-012-0175-y
47. Yu, H., Lam, W., Chen, L., Li, G., Xie, T., Wang, Q.: Neural detection of semantic code clones via tree-based convolution. In: 2019 IEEE/ACM 27th International Conference on Program Comprehension (ICPC), pp. 70–80. IEEE (2019)
48. Zager, L.A., Verghese, G.C.: Graph similarity scoring and matching. Appl. Math. Lett. **21**(1), 86–94 (2008)
49. Zhang, J., Wang, X., Zhang, H., Sun, H., Wang, K., Liu, X.: A novel neural source code representation based on abstract syntax tree. In: 2019 IEEE/ACM 41st International Conference on Software Engineering (ICSE), pp. 783–794. IEEE (2019)
50. Zhang, L., Luo, S., Pan, L., Zhouting, W., Gong, K.: FSD-CLCD: functional semantic distillation graph learning for cross-language code clone detection. Eng. Appl. Artif. Intell. **133**, 108199 (2024)

Security and Compliance

Trusted Provenance with Blockchain Technology: A Systematic Literature Review

Steven Kocadag[1], Matthias Pohl[1,2](✉), and Andreas Schreiber[2]

[1] Otto von Guericke University, Magdeburg, Germany
{steven.kocadag,matthias.pohl}@ovgu.de
[2] German Aerospace Center (DLR), Cologne, Germany
andreas.schreiber@dlr.de

Abstract. Through practices and tools that track and document the origins, evolution, and changes of software components, software development and provenance are intricately connected. The importance of provenance in the digital age has led to significant interest in using blockchain technology to store provenance data in a tamper-proof manner. This study presents an overview of current advancements in blockchain-based provenance storage research, addressing the benefits and challenges of various storage strategies. The storage types identified in the system literature review informed the development of a proprietary system. Due to the incorporation of numerous entities, activities, agents, and relationships, underlying documents can become substantially large. The study indicates that an effective approach to manage extensive data involves external storage while retaining only its fingerprint on the blockchain. This method ensures tamper-proof uploads and maintains traceability in the development process.

Keywords: Provenance · Blockchain Technology · Reliability · Software Engineering · Provenance Documents

1 Introduction

Provenance refers to the origin and historical context of an artifact, object, or data. In the digital age, the importance of provenance has increased due to the rapid creation of digital artifacts through advanced technologies and online communication. Unlike physical objects, digital artifacts can be easily copied and altered without leaving traces. Provenance facilitates the tracing of the origin and history of these digital artifacts, thereby establishing their authenticity and ownership. This is particularly critical for assets involved in research or legal matters, as well as for high-value items such as digital art and cryptocurrencies. The connection between software development and provenance is established through tools that track and document software components' origins and changes. Version control systems like Git offer a comprehensive history of

J. Fischbach et al. (Eds.): SWQD 2025, LNBIP 544, pp. 93–105, 2025.
https://doi.org/10.1007/978-3-031-89277-6_6

the codebase by recording each modification, ensuring traceability. Moreover, dependency management and build automation via Continuous Integration and Continuous Deployment (CI/CD), alongside security audits, logs, and compliance reports, significantly enhance the integrity of software components and support the framework of provenance [4,32,38]. Digital artifacts often change, while provenance records generally remain stable, as they document historical events. Altering these records compromises their value by manipulating past activities. Therefore, ensuring the quality and integrity of provenance data requires tamper-proof storage solutions. This has led to growing research interest in employing blockchain technology for this purpose. Blockchain has emerged as a transformative technology in the past decade. IBM defines it as a "shared, immutable ledger that simplifies the recording of transactions and tracking of assets." [12,30]. With its core properties of immutability and traceability, blockchain proves to be an effective means of safeguarding provenance data. While commonly associated with cryptocurrencies like Bitcoin, blockchain is increasingly being applied to diverse fields, including supply chain management, real estate, and provenance verification.

The objective of this study is to examine the use of blockchain technology for secure and tamper-proof storage of provenance data, which is defined by the PROV standard established by the World Wide Web Consortium. The PROV standard provides a framework for representing and exchanging provenance information on the Web, detailing the entities, activities, and agents involved in the creation, modification, and use of resources. Adopting the PROV standard ensures interoperability and consistency in provenance data across different systems and platforms. Therefore, the following research questions will be pursued:

What are the storage strategies for provenance information using blockchain technology according to scientific literature?

The paper at hand presents a systematic literature review [18,19] that aims to identify existing work on storing provenance information using blockchain.

2 Prerequisites

2.1 Blockchain Technology

As the development history shows, blockchain is a very young field that is subject to constant development. In the meantime, there are a large number of implementations and types that differ in their properties. Regardless of specific implementations, the following properties are attributed to blockchain [2,22,41]:

- **Decentralization**: All nodes in the network record transactions and maintain a local ledger copy, preventing single points of failure.
- **Trustlessness**: A trusted third party isn't needed to validate transactions, and nodes can transact without trusting each other. The consensus algorithm democratically validates and logs transactions.

- **Immutability**: Changing previous blocks invalidates all subsequent ones due to one-way hash functions, which complicates blockchain tampering.
- **Non-repudiation**: Transactions are signed with a private key, allowing others to verify them with the public key. They cannot be falsely initiated or denied by the sender.
- **Anonymity**: Users can communicate with the blockchain using a randomly generated address that hides their true identity
- **Transparency**: All nodes can access and verify transactions stored in the blockchain, providing public transparency.
- **Traceability**: Block headers are timestamped so that nodes can trace the origin of historical blocks.

Blockchain technology has rapidly gained attention beyond traditional tech communities. The swift adoption of new technologies often fosters heightened optimism [26]. It is essential to critically evaluate the claims regarding the capabilities of such technologies, including blockchain, as they can frequently be exaggerated.

2.2 Provenance

Traditionally, provenance has been important in determining the origin of food and art, where the source significantly affects authenticity and quality. With advances in information technology, the concept of provenance has expanded to include the tracing of information origins in various fields. The World Wide Web Consortium (W3C) has defined provenance as "information about entities, activities, and people involved in the creation of data or things that can be used to assess their quality, reliability, or trustworthiness." [1]. Furthermore, the W3C has created a standardized data model and serializations for provenance data.

In April 2013, the W3C Provenance Working Group published the PROV standard [1], replacing the prior OPM model [27]. The PROV standard includes a comprehensive framework with a model, serializations, and supporting definitions to facilitate the exchange of provenance information across diverse environments [1]. The PROV data model [28] offers formal semantics represented in various formats, including PROV-O [36], PROV-N [29], and PROV-JSON [14]. PROV-O utilizes the Web Ontology Language and RDF, while PROV-N provides a readable format with validation constraints. PROV-JSON represents the model in JSON format, enabling efficient manipulation of provenance information on the client side and facilitating effective data exchange between web services and clients.

3 Methodology

This section outlines the methodological approach used for the systematic literature review (SLR) in this research. The SLR follows three phases as established by Kitchenham [17–19]. In the planning phase, the focus of the analysis is defined, and relevant keywords and databases are selected for the search. The processing phase involves retrieving pertinent papers, conducting screening and qualitative analysis, and synthesizing findings. Finally, the results are documented in the concluding phase.

3.1 Literature Search Process

Based on the prerequisites, the search term is combined with a part related to blockchain technology and one related to provenance. As the search aims at specific solutions for the PROV standard, the search term is designed as follows:

*Title-and-Keywords (*PROV AND Blockchain) OR (Abstract(Provenance and Blockchain) AND ALL(PROV))*

The literature search has been conducted at the online libraries of Web of Science, Scopus, Science Direct and IEEE Xplore, which contain the most indexed items. Without duplicates, 33 unique articles could be retrieved in four databases.

The keyword search allows the collection of articles relevant to the specified research area. However, limitations in keyword searches may prevent the discovery of some pertinent articles. To uncover additional relevant literature, we examined the referenced works within our collection. Using the Open Citations API, we identified articles that are most frequently cited, focusing on those mentioned at least three times. Besides standardization documents from W3C and Hyperledger Fabric, we also included two additional articles not previously in our collection.

3.2 Study Selection

Following the collection of search results, a systematic selection of works for analysis is conducted within the systematic literature review (SLR) framework. Specific inclusion criteria are established, encompassing basic characteristics such as availability and language, along with content-related requirements addressing provenance standards and blockchain technology. These criteria serve as indicators of relevance and quality. A study must be accessible (1) to a diverse audience, ensuring clarity for individuals with varying expertise. It should be available in English or German (2), with the potential for additional language support to improve accessibility. Furthermore, a study must encode provenance information according to W3C Prov or similar standards to ensure data transparency (3). Additionally, the provenance model should either be stored on a blockchain for secure record-keeping or include a theoretical framework for implementing such storage using blockchain technology (4). Due to our study selection criteria, we had to eliminate 15 studies and continue our SLR with 20 remaining studies.

3.3 Data Extraction

According to Kitchenham, in the data extraction phase, all the information from the selected papers that is needed to answer the scientific question is processed [19]. To identify existing works that use blockchain technology to store PROV-related documents, we use the following analysis structure.

- **Goal:** What are the aims of the study?
- **Application area:** What's the domain of the entities that provenance is tracked (e.g., Medicine or Finance)?
- **Blockchain:** What blockchain is used?
- **Provenance Standard:** How is provenance information encoded?
- **Provenance Data Generation:** How is provenance data created?
- **Blockchain Storage:** How is provenance data stored on the blockchain?

The initial step in our SLR is to identify the objectives of each study. Understanding the overall goals is vital, as it justifies the research's ambition and methodology, and informs related areas such as the blockchain technology used and access permissions. We categorize the findings by extracting each study's scope, highlighting common areas for storing provenance information on the blockchain. Furthermore, we focus on the specific blockchain technologies used, which helps identify prevalent platforms. We also analyze the encoding methods for provenance information and document any procedures for generating documents that do not adhere to the PROV standard. Lastly, we examine the various storage methods on the blockchain to enable a comparative analysis of approaches.

4 Literature Analysis

This literature review examined a total of 20 studies that mainly propose systems for tracking and storing provenance information using blockchain technology. The studies explored different blockchain platforms, such as Hyperledger Fabric and Ethereum, and different W3C PROV-related provenance standards, such as SWPROV and OPM. Among 20 studies, out of which 16 named the blockchain network they used, 11 choose Hyperledger. The authors highlight Hyperledger Fabric's modular architecture as a key factor in their decision [8–10]. This architecture grants flexibility in configuring and plugging in components, making it well-suited for use in industries such as banking, finance, and health insurance that require frequent innovation and flexible domain logic. Additionally, the authors point out that Hyperledger Fabric uses general-purpose programming languages (GPL) such as Java, Go, and Nodejs, which makes it more accessible and easier for developers to work with compared to other platforms that use domain-specific-languages (DSL). Finally, the authors mention that

Table 1. Overview of Blockchain Technologies and Provenance Standard in Scientific Literature

	W3C PROV	OPM	Modified/Individual
Hyperledger Fabric	[8–10,23]	[37]	[5,11,15,24,25,39]
Ethereum	[35]	[31]	[3]
Other	[13,16,20,34]		[21,33]

Hyperledger Fabric is a permissioned blockchain platform, which is essential for organizations that want to keep their data private and should not be exposed to public audiences. Besides Hyperledger Fabric and Ethereum, Tendermint and Tieron API are used. The application areas are broadly distributed across Open Data, Food Delivery, Internet of Things, and Healthcare. An overview is provided in Table 1. In a study by Kirstein [16], requirements for a system to track and store provenance data in linked open data were defined, guided by the W3C PROV standard. While next steps for development were outlined, they have not yet been implemented. Hogan and Helfert [13] explored the theoretical application of distributed ledger technology (DLT) for tracking and storing provenance data. They mapped W3C PROV components to blockchain elements and assessed the alignment between the PROV data model and Bitcoin's implementation. A key finding is that data provenance instances relying on circular reference relationships may be unimplementable on a blockchain. Ioni and Pahl [15] propose a blockchain architecture to track identities and provenance of business network orchestration decisions using the W3C PROV standard. They implement PROV components as smart contract classes, mapping entities to assets, agents to participants, and activities to transactions. Similarly, Fadhel et al. [11] adapted PROV-N to model IoT attacks, storing documents in Hyperledger Fabric's keystore. Markovic et al. [24,25] used provenance to track food deliveries by storing FS-PROV data in smart contracts accessible via a RESTful API [25]. They employed an EP-PLAN ontology, which extends the PROV model for linking plans [25]. Similarly, Dang and Anh [9] stored data in five smart contracts to form provenance information, synchronizing with the Open Data Platform to update object properties, thereby creating a new "chapter" of provenance with each action. Dang and Duong [8] utilize the W3C PROV standard to monitor changes in open data, storing the dataset's URL and checksum on the blockchain. Similarly, Song et al. [34] focus on provenance tracking and sharing, incorporating a person's identity signature and operation details within the blockchain to prevent tampering. They map elements like Assets, Actions, and Initiators to W3C PROV's Entities, Activities, and Agents. In the field of healthcare, Margheri et al. [23] utilize the W3C PROV standard to investigate data provenance, treating health documents as Entities within PROV documentation. Their approach involves canonicalizing PROV documents and storing key-value pairs of document hashes and provenance information in a blockchain. Similarly, Lautert et al. [20] focus on fog computing, employing the W3C PROV standard to store provenance information in private blockchains for each fog node, which is later shared with a global blockchain. Sigwart et al. [33] propose a framework for tracking provenance in IoT systems, utilizing a data provenance model and blockchain storage [33]. It consists of a storage layer for low-level provenance data, a generic layer for general functionality, and a specific layer for use case customization. Demichev introduced PROVHL, a decentralized data management system using Hyperledger Fabric and an adapted W3C PROV standard [10]. This system stores key-value pairs of assets like files on the blockchain, mapping assets, transactions, and participants to the adapted W3C

PROV elements. Zhang et al. [40] proposed a system for managing provenance data in power grids using Hyperledger Fabric and a modified PROV standard. It involves three smart contracts: one for data access, one for data logging, and one for data provenance. The data logging contract establishes a provenance chain based on activities like initialization and deletion, while the data provenance contract retrieves the operation log to form a complete provenance chain. Recent studies highlight the challenges of storing provenance data directly on the blockchain. Bose et al. [3] note that the costs of storage on platforms like Ethereum can be prohibitive for data-intensive applications. Additionally, Sun et al. [35] point out that provenance data often exceeds block limits or contains sensitive information restricted to specific users. As a result, alternative storage solutions are being explored. Liang et al. [21] proposed ProvChain, a system that uses the Tierion API to track cloud operations while storing provenance data in a database. The system generates data records containing information such as the operation's date and time, the user's username, the affected file's name, and the action taken. These records are published to the blockchain using the Chainpoint standard, which combines the hashes into a Merkle tree.

Table 2. Overview of PROV Storage Strategies

	Document-wise	Canonicalized	Element-wise	Subgraphs
On-Chain	[11,20,24,25]	[23]	[9,10,15,33,34,40]	
Ofsf-Chain	[3,8,31,37]		[6,21]	[35]

Ramachandran and Kantarcioglu [31] introduced a system in knowledge management that leverages Ethereum for data provenance collection and verification. It employs the Open Provenance Model (OPM), representing provenance as a triplet of agents, artifacts, and processes. The system features a Document Tracker that logs change events and stores OPM data in a database. Tunstadt et al. [37] proposed a framework for tracking data provenance using the Open Provenance Model. It stores on-chain data such as checksums, editors, operations, ownership, and pointers, while off-chain data includes the actual content. Bose et al. proposed a system for software provenance that employs Ethereum to capture and analyze provenance data [3]. Using the SWProcess Specification, the system generates provenance data from review data, storing critical PROV Data and its hashes on the blockchain while keeping full PROV data in an Off-Chain database. They also recommend using cryptographic distributed databases like IPFS for storing complete provenance data. Coelho et al. [5] recommend a system for capturing, storing, and analyzing provenance-related data in collaborative research. The system uses ProvONE (PROV for scientific workflows) as the provenance standard. Sun et al. [35] proposed a system for sharing provenance data via Ethereum and the W3C PROV standard. The system partitions the PROV graph into subgraphs using a BFS-based method, encrypts them, and uploads them to the blockchain. Users can retrieve and compose these subgraphs into a new graph, with the provenance subgraphs and access control policies stored on-chain, while transaction and block information remains off-chain.

5 Comparison of Storage Strategies

The SLR has explored various strategies for storing provenance information using blockchain. To determine the most suitable approach for our needs, we will summarize and critically evaluate these methods in terms of their benefits and drawbacks for storing and retrieving W3C PROV documents. The primary distinction among approaches lies in data storage methods: some store data directly on the blockchain, while others only keep a hash on-chain and link to an external database or URL for the actual data. Additionally, there are variations in how provenance data is structured, with options to store entire W3C PROV documents and their hashes or to break them down into elements like entities and activities, capturing their interrelationships. We will categorize these approaches based on the location and structure of the stored data in Table 2. Current research predominantly emphasizes the storage of provenance data within smart contracts on the blockchain. Storing data **on-chain** presents several advantages, as outlined in Table 3. On-chain data is immutable and cannot be altered once stored, thereby enhancing trust and transparency. In decentralized networks, this data is replicated across all nodes, eliminating single points of failure and ensuring availability as long as the network operates. Furthermore, on-chain data benefits from high resistance to tampering and hacking attempts compared to traditional databases. However, the transparency of on-chain data storage raises privacy concerns, particularly for sensitive information, which may be exposed to other participants. Additionally, there are two major drawbacks-speed and cost. Blockchains exhibit slow write speeds and can lag in data retrieval; consequently, even low-performance databases may outperform them. In public blockchains, writing data incurs fees In cost-sensitive scenarios, it is often impractical to store excessive data on-chain. As a result, many approaches advocate for **off-chain** data storage in traditional databases or the InterPlanetary File System (IPFS), allowing the blockchain to retain only the hash value alongside a reference, such as an ID, URL, or IPFS address. This method mitigates the downsides of on-chain solutions by improving scalability, speed, cost-effectiveness, and facilitating controlled access to data. Despite these advantages, off-chain storage presents risks, especially concerning data tampering. While hashes can help ensure data integrity, an attacker's ability to modify data without detection remains a concern. The prominent hash function SHA-256 provides strong security, as generating a document with an identical hash is exceedingly difficult due to its vast possible values. Nevertheless, using centralized databases for off-chain storage creates a single point of failure, undermining the decentralized security of the blockchain. While the blockchain can signal tampering, it cannot restore compromised data.

Table 3. Comparison of Storage Methods: On-Chain vs Off-Chain

	On-Chain	Off-Chain
Immutability	✓	○
Decentralization	✓	○
Data Integrity	✓	✓
Cost	−	+
Speed	−	+
Privacy	○	✓

When analyzing the structure of stored provenance documents, significant distinctions arise between document-wise and element-wise storage, as summarized in Table 4. **Document-wise** storage and canonicalized documents are grouped together due to their similar properties, while element-wise storage and subgraphs form a second group. Storing a document in its entirety is straightforward and requires minimal computational effort, making it suitable primarily for smaller graphs. However, this on-chain storage approach is generally inefficient. In contrast, **element-wise** storage requires greater computational resources, as individual identities or subgraphs must be disclosed and stored separately, along with their relationships, to enable future reconstruction. This method can enhance efficiency in on-chain contexts by allowing the reuse of components across multiple documents, which avoids redundancy. However, off-chain storage necessitates the retention of numerous references and hashes to realize the benefits of element-wise storage, increasing the total number of stored hashes relative to the number of elements. Thus, while element-wise storage can reduce blockchain data load in on-chain scenarios, it may increase off-chain storage complexity. In cases of off-chain tampering, element-wise storage allows for tracking modifications to specific elements, a feature absent in document-wise storage. Additionally, the risk of tampering is higher in document-wise storage, as it involves a single hash, whereas element-wise storage's multiple hashes complicate meaningful content alteration.

Table 4. Comparison of Storage Methods: Document-based and Element-based

	Document-based	Element-based
Computational Effort	-	+
On-Chain Storage Cost	++	+
Off-Chain Storage Cost	-	-
Off-Chain Diff	✗	✓
Tamper Risk	-	-

6 Conclusion

This paper presents an overview of current advancements in blockchain-based provenance storage research, addressing the benefits and challenges of various storage strategies. The storage types identified in the SLR informed the development of a proprietary system. Due to the incorporation of numerous entities, activities, agents, and relationships, underlying documents can become substantially large. The SLR indicates that an effective approach to manage extensive data involves external storage while retaining only its fingerprint on the blockchain. This method ensures tamper-proof uploads and maintains traceability in the development process. A certifier keeps a copy of the original document, allowing for the reproduction of the development workflow and exportation of associated provenance files, making it sufficient to store just the fingerprint, thereby safeguarding the provenance data from public access. Additionally, the SLR discusses storing W3C PROVs on either a document or element basis. Each execution generates a provenance record that includes the hash of the entire workflow. This enhances security and requires multiple hashes to be compromised to affect integrity. By retaining components of the development workflow, the system can accurately identify tampered components and provide certifiers with reliable information. It should be noted that semantically equivalent provenance documents can yield different hashes due to special characters or variations in element order. To address this, PROV documents are canonicalized before hashing [23]. Since the input data is in PROV-JSON format, the JSON canonicalization scheme is applied, which creates a unified representation by sorting JSON object properties, facilitating the exchange of JSON data "as is." [7].

References

1. PROV-Overview. An Overview of the PROV Family of Documents. Project report (April 2013). https://eprints.soton.ac.uk/356854/
2. Bashir, I.: Mastering blockchain: a deep dive into distributed ledgers, consensus protocols, smart contracts, DApps, cryptocurrencies, Ethereum, and more. Birmingham Mumbai, third edition edn, Expert insight, Packt (2020)
3. Bose, R.J.C., Phokela, K.K., Kaulgud, V., Podder, S.: BLINKER: a Blockchain-Enabled Framework for Software Provenance. In: 26th Asia-Pacific Software Engineering Conference (APSEC). IEEE, Putrajaya, Malaysia (2019). https://doi.org/10.1109/APSEC48747.2019.00010
4. Buneman, P., Khanna, S., Wang-Chiew, T.: Why and where: a characterization of data provenance. In: Van den Bussche, J., Vianu, V. (eds.) ICDT 2001. LNCS, vol. 1973, pp. 316–330. Springer, Heidelberg (2001). https://doi.org/10.1007/3-540-44503-X_20
5. Coelho, R., Braga, R., David, J., Dantas, M., Ströele, V., Campos, F.: Integrating blockchain for data sharing and collaboration support in scientific ecosystem platform, pp. 264–273 (2021). https://doi.org/10.24251/HICSS.2021.031

6. Coelho, R., Braga, R., David, J., Stroele, V., Campos, F., Dantas, M.: A Blockchain-Based Architecture for Trust in Collaborative Scientific Experimentation. J. Grid Comput, **20**(4) (2022), https://doi.org/10.1007/s10723-022-09626-x
7. Cyberphone: JSON-Canonicalization Scheme (JCS) (2019). https://github.com/cyberphone/json-canonicalization
8. Dang, T., Duong, T.: An effective and elastic blockchain-based provenance preserving solution for the open data. Inter. J. Web Inform. Syst. **17**(5), 480–515 (2021). https://doi.org/10.1108/IJWIS-03-2021-0029
9. Dang, T.K., Anh, T.D.: A pragmatic blockchain based solution for managing provenance and characteristics in the open data context. In: Dang, T.K., Küng, J., Takizawa, M., Chung, T.M. (eds.) FDSE 2020. LNCS, vol. 12466, pp. 221–242. Springer, Cham (2020). https://doi.org/10.1007/978-3-030-63924-2_13
10. Demichev, A., Kryukov, A., Prikhod'ko, N.: Business process engineering for data storing and processing in a collaborative distributed environment based on provenance metadata, smart contracts and blockchain technology. J. Grid Comput. **19**(1), 1–30 (2021). https://doi.org/10.1007/s10723-021-09544-4
11. Fadhel, N., Lombardi, F., Aniello, L., Margheri, A., Sassone, V.: Towards a semantic modelling for threat analysis of IoT applications: a case study on transactive energy, vol. 2019 (2019). https://doi.org/10.1049/cp.2019.0147
12. Gupta, M.: Blockchain for dummies. John Wiley & Sons, Inc., Hoboken, NJ, 2nd ibm limited edition edn. (2018). oCLC: 1066258248
13. Hogan, G., Helfert, M.: Transparent cloud privacy: data provenance expression in blockchain, pp. 430–436 (2019). https://doi.org/10.5220/0007733404300436
14. Huynh, T.D., Jewell, M., Keshavarz, A., Michaelides, D., Yang, H., Moreau, L.: The PROV-JSON Serialization (2013). https://www.w3.org/Submission/prov-json/
15. Ioini, N., Pahl, C.: Trustworthy orchestration of container based edge computing using permissioned blockchain, pp. 147–154 (2018). https://doi.org/10.1109/IoTSMS.2018.8554470
16. Kirstein, F.: A decentralized provenance network for linked open data. **2548**, 104–115 (2019)
17. Kitchenham, B.: Systematic reviews. In: 10th International Symposium on Software Metrics 2004, Proceedings, pp. xii–xii (2004). https://doi.org/10.1109/METRIC.2004.1357885
18. Kitchenham, B.: Procedures for performing systematic reviews. Technical Report TR-SE-0401, Department of Computer Science, Keele University, UK (2004)
19. Kitchenham, B.A., Charters, S.: Guidelines for performing systematic literature reviews in software engineering. Tech. Rep. EBSE 2007-001, Keele University and Durham University Joint Report (July 2007)
20. Lautert, F., Pigatto, D., Gomes, L.: A fog architecture for privacy-preserving data provenance using blockchains, vol. 2020 (July 2020). https://doi.org/10.1109/ISCC50000.2020.9219724
21. Liang, X., Shetty, S., Tosh, D., Kamhoua, C., Kwiat, K., Njilla, L.: ProvChain: a blockchain-based data provenance architecture in cloud environment with enhanced privacy and availability. In: 17th IEEE/ACM International Symposium on Cluster, Cloud and Grid Computing. IEEE, Madrid, Spain (2017). https://doi.org/10.1109/CCGRID.2017.8
22. Liang, Y.-C.: Blockchain for dynamic spectrum management. In: Dynamic Spectrum Management. SCT, pp. 121–146. Springer, Singapore (2020). https://doi.org/10.1007/978-981-15-0776-2_5

23. Margheri, A., Masi, M., Miladi, A., Sassone, V., Rosenzweig, J.: Decentralised provenance for healthcare data. Int. J. Med. Inform. **141**, 104197 (2020). https://doi.org/10.1016/j.ijmedinf.2020.104197
24. Markovic, M., Edwards, P., Jacobs, N.: Recording Provenance of Food Delivery Using IoT, Semantics and Business Blockchain Networks, pp. 116–118 (2019). https://doi.org/10.1109/IOTSMS48152.2019.8939250
25. Markovic, M., Jacobs, N., Dryja, K., Edwards, P., Strachan, N.: Integrating internet of things, provenance, and blockchain to enhance trust in last mile food deliveries. Front. Sustainable Food Sys, **4** (2020). https://doi.org/10.3389/fsufs.2020.563424
26. Mitchell, M.: Why AI is harder than we think. In: Proceedings of the Genetic and Evolutionary Computation Conference. ACM (2021). https://doi.org/10.1145/3449639.3465421
27. Moreau, L., Freire, J., Futrelle, J., McGrath, R.E., Myers, J., Paulson, P.: The open provenance model: an overview. In: Freire, J., Koop, D., Moreau, L. (eds.) IPAW 2008. LNCS, vol. 5272, pp. 323–326. Springer, Heidelberg (2008). https://doi.org/10.1007/978-3-540-89965-5_31
28. Moreau, L., Missier, P.: PROV-DM: The PROV Data Model. https://www.w3.org/TR/2013/REC-prov-dm-20130430/
29. Moreau, L., Missier, P.: PROV-N: The Provenance Notation (2013). https://www.w3.org/TR/2013/REC-prov-n-20130430/
30. Pohl, M., Degenkolbe, R., Staegemann, D., Turowski, K.: Towards a blockchain technology framework–literature review on components in blockchain implementations. In: ACIS 2020 Proceedings (2020)
31. Ramachandran, A., Kantarcioglu, M.: SmartProvenance: a distributed, blockchain based dataprovenance system. In: Proceedings of the Eighth ACM Conference on Data and Application Security and Privacy. ACM, Tempe AZ USA (2018). https://doi.org/10.1145/3176258.3176333
32. Schreiber, A., von Kurnatowski, L., de Boer, C.: Analyzing software engineering processes with provenance-based knowledge graphs. In: IEEE Aerospace Conference (50100). IEEE (2021)
33. Sigwart, M., Borkowski, M., Peise, M., Schulte, S., Tai, S.: A secure and extensible blockchain-based data provenance framework for the Internet of Things. Pers. Ubiquit. Comput. (1), 1–15 (2020). https://doi.org/10.1007/s00779-020-01417-z
34. Song, Z., et al.: An improved data provenance framework integrating blockchain and PROV model. In: International Conference on Computer Science and Management Technology (ICCSMT). IEEE, Shanghai, China (2020). https://doi.org/10.1109/ICCSMT51754.2020.00073
35. Sun, L.S., Bai, X., Zhang, C., Li, Y., Zhang, Y.B., Guo, W.Q.: BSTProv: blockchain-based secure and trustworthy data provenance sharing. Electronics **11**(9), 1489 (2022). https://doi.org/10.3390/electronics11091489
36. Timothy Lebo, S.S., McGuinness, D.: PROV-O: The PROV Ontology (2013). https://www.w3.org/TR/2013/REC-prov-o-20130430/
37. Tunstad, P., Khan, A., Ha, P.: HyperProv: decentralized resilient data provenance at the edge with blockchains (2019). https://doi.org/10.1145/3366627.3368105
38. Xu, P., Sengupta, A.: Provenance in software engineering-a configuration management view. In: AMCIS 2005 Proceedings, p. 515 (2005)
39. Zhang, X., Feng, J., Yin, Z., Lin, J.: Trusted query method for data provenance based on blockchain. Yingyong Kexue Xuebao/J. Appli. Sci. **39**(1), 42–54 (2021). https://doi.org/10.3969/j.issn.0255-8297.2021.01.004

40. Zhang, Z., et al.: Research on consistency tracing technology of dispatching control model data based on blockchain. In: IEEE 5th Advanced Information Technology, Electronic and Automation Control Conference. IEEE, Chongqing, China (2021). https://doi.org/10.1109/IAEAC50856.2021.9390682
41. Zheng, Z., Xie, S., Dai, H., Chen, X., Wang, H.: An overview of blockchain technology: architecture, consensus, and future trends. In: IEEE International Congress on Big Data. IEEE, Honolulu, HI, USA (2017). https://doi.org/10.1109/BigDataCongress.2017.85

Academic-Industry Collaborations

Experiences Applying Lean R&D in Industry-Academia Collaboration Projects

Marcos Kalinowski(✉), Lucas Romao, Ariane Rodrigues, Clarissa Barbosa, Hugo Villamizar, Simone D. J. Barbosa, and Hélio Lopes

Pontifical Catholic University of Rio de Janeiro (PUC-Rio), Rio de Janeiro, RJ 22451-900, Brazil
{kalinowski,lromao,arodrigues,cbarbosa,hvillamizar, simone,lopes}@inf.puc-rio.br

Abstract. Lean R&D has been used at PUC-Rio to foster industry-academia collaboration in innovation projects across multiple sectors. This industrial experience paper describes recent experiences and evaluation results from applying Lean R&D in partnership with Petrobras in the oil and gas sector and Americanas in retail. The findings highlight Lean R&D's effectiveness in transforming ideas into meaningful business outcomes. Based on responses from 57 participants—including team members, managers, and sponsors—the assessment indicates that stakeholders find the structured phases of Lean R&D well-suited to innovation projects and endorse the approach. Although acknowledging that successful collaboration relies on various factors, this industrial experience positions Lean R&D as a promising framework for industry-academia projects focused on achieving rapid, impactful results for industry partners.

Keywords: Lean R&D · Industry-Academia Collaboration · Innovation · Software Engineering

1 Introduction

Industry-Academia Collaboration (IAC) projects have been a main focus at PUC-Rio, Latin America's leading university in industry income according to the Times Higher Education ranking [13]. Several of these IAC projects are carried out within the oil and gas industry, mainly motivated by the needs of Petrobras, a state-owned Brazilian multinational corporation headquartered in Rio de Janeiro, Brazil.

Research, Development, and Innovation (RDI) initiatives in the oil and gas industry commonly involve cooperation terms with research institutes and universities. These terms were usually designed in a plan-driven manner, with deliveries that, given research uncertainties, typically spanned several years. In

J. Fischbach et al. (Eds.): SWQD 2025, LNBIP 544, pp. 109–123, 2025.
https://doi.org/10.1007/978-3-031-89277-6_7

September 2019, representatives of Petrobras came up with a challenge: to structure an RDI collaboration that would enable agile deliveries of Minimal Viable Products (MVPs) to test business hypotheses, allowing to take ideas from their conception to impact.

To address this challenge, we designed an RDI approach to allow fast-paced MVP deliveries. The resulting approach, inspired by continuous software engineering principles [2] and concepts from Lean [9] and Lean Startup [10], was called Lean R&D [5,6]. In January 2020, Petrobras started four IAC projects with PUC-Rio applying Lean R&D. The ExACTa (exacta.inf.puc-rio.br) laboratory was created at PUC-Rio to handle such agile RDI projects, aiming at fast-paced deliveries of R&D projects, aligning research on artificial intelligence, human-computer interaction, and software engineering with the digital transformation needs of industrial partners.

The first case studies on using Lean R&D provided initial indications into the feasibility of using the approach within RDI projects [6,12]. Since then, ExACTa has been using Lean R&D to deliver innovative solutions to several industry partners. This industrial experience paper provides new results assessing the use of Lean R&D in more recent RDI IAC projects with Petrobras and Americanas, a player active in the retail business in Brazil, which owns more than 1,000 physical stores spread throughout the country. We report on the experiences and their results, assess the perception of the suitability of Lean R&D, and discuss the overall acceptance from the point of view of members of the R&D teams, business and technical managers, and sponsors.

With Petrobras, we focus on the use of Lean R&D in two Artificial Intelligence (AI) projects. Both were subject to patent applications [7,8] and received a Petrobras inventor award at the end of 2022. One of these projects, called Smart Tocha (*Smart Torch*), comprises an AI solution that continuously processes oil refinery torch burn images to automatically act over refinery controls to increase the energy efficiency of the gas burning. The other one, called Inspetor Digital (*Digital Inspector*), involves using AI to help refinery equipment inspectors complete reports more quickly and efficiently. This paper focuses on the process used at ExACTa, not on the particular projects; more details on the projects can be found within the patent applications.

Americanas started their IAC with ExACTa in July 2022 and set up four teams to simultaneously handle RDI projects using Lean R&D. These projects concerned innovating the management of physical stores, improving logistic operations, and applying machine learning for product classification and e-commerce recommendations. While ExACTa R&D employees working on the projects for Petrobras were experienced professionals, Americanas wanted to involve undergrad, master, and Ph.D. students in the teams. The contract involved applying two complete Lean R&D cycles throughout one year (six months for each MVP delivery per team).

Each team had ten members: eight undergraduate students, one master's student, and one PhD student. The team was supported by a general coordination involving representatives of ExACTa and Americanas and a dedicated mentor with a Ph.D. in computer science. The students also received training and mentorship from researchers of PUC-Rio. We called these teams ExACTa FIT, where FIT is a Portuguese acronym standing for education in technological innovation. The ExACTa FIT teams conducted all Lean R&D phases, including ideating innovative solutions.

We report on the outcomes of these projects and perceptions on Lean R&D gathered through questionnaires applied to the different stakeholders at Petrobras and Americanas. We received 57 responses, mainly indicating the suitability of the Lean R&D's phases and its overall acceptance, but also providing attention points related to the ease of learning and applying the approach and improvement opportunities.

2 Overview of Lean R&D

When designing the Lean R&D approach, the main requirements were to allow maximizing business value while minimizing waste, allowing to fail fast to enable handling opportunities, and enabling to address complex RDI problems with fast-paced deliveries.

Based on these requirements, the approach was designed starting with a Lean Inception [1] ideation workshop, parallel (early) technical feasibility assessment and conception phases, scrum-based development, and continuous experimentation. An overview of Lean R&D is shown in Fig. 1.

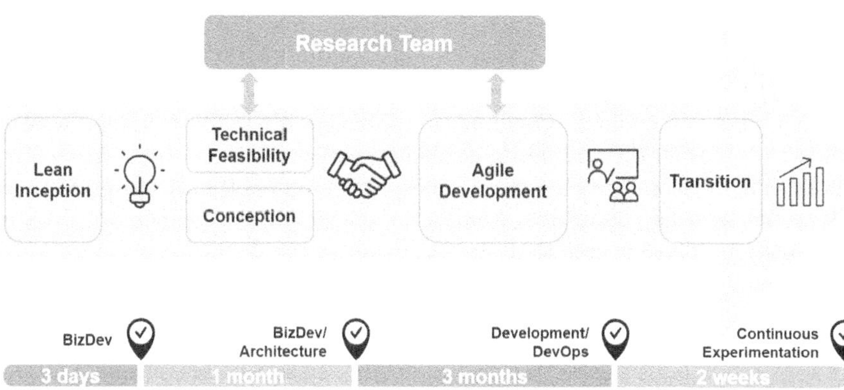

Fig. 1. Overview of the Lean R&D approach. The timeline is illustrative and reflects typical timeframes used within the ExACTa PUC-Rio laboratory.

It is possible to observe four checkpoints, a set of activities, and the support of a dedicated research team for technical solution-related activities. More details on these elements and the involved roles can be found in our previous paper describing Lean R&D [6]. Hereafter, we summarise the activities to provide an overview understanding.

The approach starts with a *Lean Inception* to allow stakeholders to jointly outline the vision of an MVP that can be used to test business hypotheses associated with industrial impact. This phase emphasizes co-creation between academic and industry teams, ensuring alignment on the MVP's objectives and expected outcomes.

At the first checkpoint, a steering committee (including the sponsor customer) must approve the MVP outline and its intended business value. Otherwise, if the idea of the MVP or its expected results are not promising enough, it fails fast, and a new Lean Inception is conducted, potentially focusing on a different business problem. This checkpoint thus ensures that only high-potential projects move forward, optimizing resource allocation and focus.

In the *Technical Feasibility* phase, the development team, assisted by the research team, starts investigating the technical feasibility of implementing the features identified during the Lean Inception. In parallel, the *Conception* involves a Product Owner (PO) detailing the MVP features identified during the Lean Inception by applying product backlog-building co-creation dynamics and other typical agile requirements elicitation and specification techniques (e.g., user stories with acceptance criteria). A UX/UI designer also details the MVP's user experience and user interface in this phase, ensuring a clear design direction.

The second checkpoint involves the steering committee analyzing the requirements specification, mainly based on the UI prototype and the results of the technical feasibility assessment, to decide whether the MVP should proceed to development. This checkpoint helps to prevent investments in technically challenging solutions that may not yield the desired business outcomes.

Thereafter, the *Agile Development* phase involves the development team, with the support of the research team, implementing the MVP following Scrum ceremonies. Customer representatives are expected to actively participate in the sprint planning and reviews, providing continuous feedback and helping the team to align closely with the end user's needs and expectations.

Following development, the third checkpoint requires the PO to present the MVP to the steering committee, where they decide on its readiness for production transition. This ensures that the MVP meets the defined criteria for value and functionality before entering the market.

Finally, the *Transition* phase involves the development and infrastructure team preparing the MVP for beta testing in its final environment, where continuous experimentation approaches are applied to assess the MVP's effectiveness in confirming the business hypotheses.

The last checkpoint focuses on evaluating continuous experimentation results to determine whether the business hypotheses were validated and if future investment in additional MVP increments is justified. This data-driven approach helps in making informed decisions for scaling or adapting the MVP based on real-world outcomes.

3 Applying Lean R&D

We analyze the application of Lean R&D to characterize the approach with respect to its suitability for RDI IAC projects and its general acceptance from the point of view of the teams, the business and technical managers from the customer side, and customer sponsors. Beyond describing the application outcomes, we applied a questionnaire to the different stakeholders to support our analyses, with questions focusing on the suitability of the Lean R&D phases and the overall approach acceptance. The questionnaires and anonymized raw data can be found at https://doi.org/10.5281/zenodo.8317454.

From the two projects with Petrobras, we received a total of 15 responses (out of 19 invitations): twelve from the ExACTa R&D team members (ten from ExACta and two from Petrobras working as POs), two from technical managers of Petrobras, and one from the main sponsor of the artificial intelligence in refinery operation projects. They were highly experienced, with a minimum experience of four years and a median of eight years, and covered all the roles involved in the Lean R&D approach in both projects. The technical managers and sponsor answered separate questionnaires more objectively focused on the method's acceptance.

From the projects with Americanas, we received a total of 42 responses (out of 48 invitations): 38 from the ExACTa FIT team members, one from a technical manager of Americanas, one from a business manager of Americanas, and two from the sponsors responsible for Americanas' digital innovation projects. They were much less experienced (students, including MS and Ph.D. students), with a minimum and median experience of one year. They also cover the roles involved in the Lean R&D approach. As done for Petrobras, again the technical managers and sponsors answered a separate questionnaire focused on the method's acceptance.

4 Lessons Learned

4.1 Lean R&D Application Outcomes

In both experiences, Lean R&D enabled defining joined MVP visions, addressing research-related uncertainties early (in the technical feasibility phase), and efficiently delivering valuable MVPs. The two projects delivered to Petrobras resulted in international patent applications [7,8] and received a Petrobras inventor award at the end of 2022.

The Smart Tocha project, according to continuous experimentation measurements, results in energy savings comparable to the energy consumption of a city with 20,000 inhabitants per refinery. Petrobras mainly uses the SAFe [11] scaled agile framework for software development projects, and the Smart Tocha MVP was loaded into a SAFe agile release train with the mission of rolling it out to several refineries. It is noteworthy that Lean R&D aims to deliver innovative MVPs, not to sustain or evolve them, for which other approaches (such as SAFe) may be employed.

The Digital Inspector MVP was also successfully delivered. It was integrated into Petrobras' equipment inspection system and, based on continuous experimentation measurements, is helping refinery equipment inspectors to complete reports more quickly and efficiently.

On the overall suitability of Lean R&D for innovation projects, the sponsor at Petrobras mentioned his satisfaction with the fast-paced deliveries and business results in the questionnaire: "Lean R&D is appropriate for research and development innovation projects; it sped up the deliveries and business results. Furthermore, it avoids wasting effort on projects that are not promising."

With respect to Americanas, the MVPs were delivered as scheduled in January and July 2023 and are also positively impacting the business. Unfortunately, we have no continuous experimentation results at hand yet. One of the sponsors answered that "Lean R&D was very appropriate for the projects, not just because it made them agile, but mainly because it placed all participants as protagonists in understanding the problem, ideating the solution and building the MVP, fundamental steps to favor innovative solutions." The other sponsor answered "The Lean R&D approach helped to structure the innovation projects, from conception to development, providing a methodology for integrating the business areas and the research and development teams."

The satisfaction with the project can also be perceived in a public communication made by the company in its LinkedIn profile (with more than one million followers): "The project aimed to allow students to find solutions to real-world problems and enrich their training, combining it with graduate-level research and direct exposure to the company's specific challenges. The projects were carried out with great efficiency and dedication by the students and the professors from PUC-Rio in partnership with the business areas and the digital innovation area of Americanas."

4.2 Suitability of the Lean R&D Phases

We analyzed the answers of the Petrobras and Americanas teams regarding their agreement on the suitability of each phase with respect to its purpose. We used a five-point Likert scale (totally disagree, partially disagree, neutral, partially agree, and totally agree). The results for the ExACTa R&D team working with Petrobras and the ExACTa FIT team working with Americanas are shown in Figs. 2 and 3.

As shown in Fig. 2, in the more experienced R&D team working with Petrobras, three out of twelve team members partially disagreed that Lean Inceptions are suitable for identifying business hypotheses. Two of them justified their answers. They explained that Lean Inception is concerned with outlining the MVP and describing related business hypotheses but not identifying them, which might require analyzing the business. Indeed, they precisely highlighted that the main purpose of Lean Inception is focused on outlining the MVP to deliver business value.

As shown in Fig. 3, in the team working with Americanas, one of the 38 participants partially disagreed on the suitability of the conception phase for

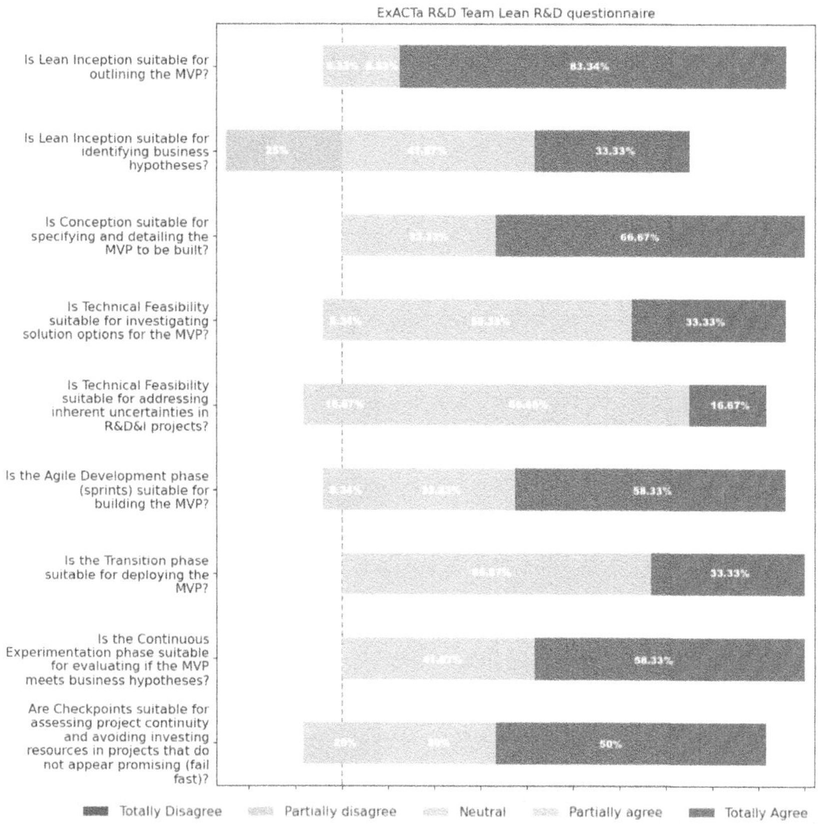

Fig. 2. Suitability of Lean R&D phases according to the ExACTa R&D team working with Petrobras.

detailing the MVP. However, the justification only pointed to difficulties in conducting the conception phase. This same participant also partially disagreed on the technical feasibility, together with one other, who questioned the support of this phase for addressing uncertainties. Based on their comments, they were actually referring to problems within their team, which did not get sufficient stakeholder involvement. Furthermore, one participant disagreed on the suitability of the continuous experimentation phase. Mainly, this participant was worried about end-users using an MVP with an extremely limited set of features. While this might indeed be a risk, this aspect forces the focus on the main features to add value.

Finally, two participants disagreed on the importance of the checkpoints, and one partially disagreed. However, based on their justifications, they did not understand the purpose of these checkpoints. One of them mentioned that the checkpoints are insufficient to communicate all project-related problems.

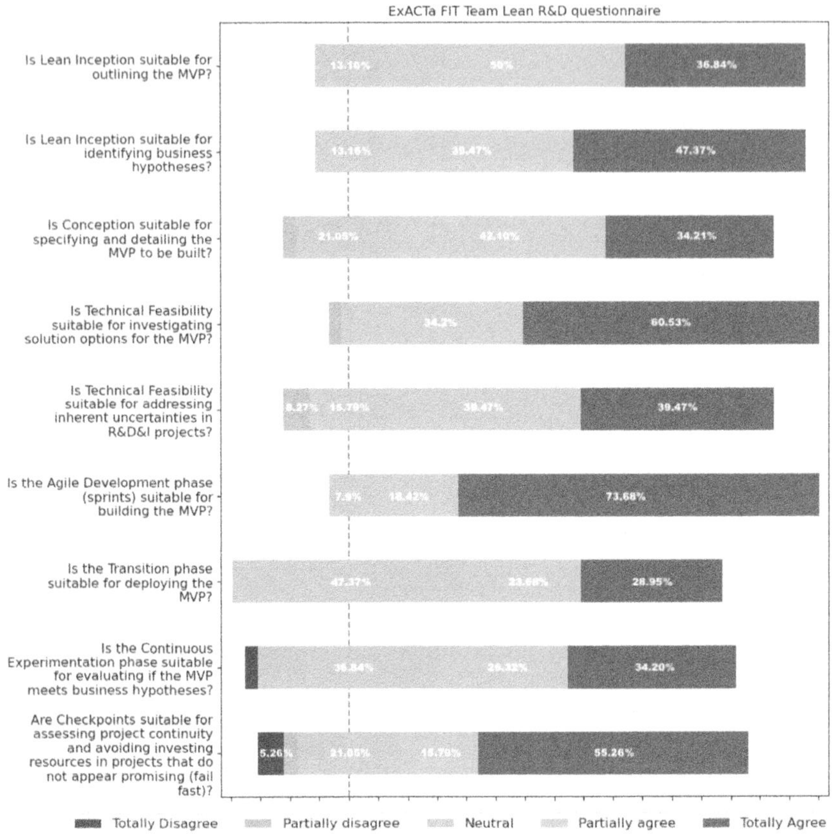

Fig. 3. Suitability of Lean R&D phases according to the ExACTa FIT team working with Americanas.

The other one mentioned that changes can happen at every sprint planning. Discussing strategic innovation decisions in every sprint is typically not feasible.

Both figures mainly indicate an agreement on the suitability of the Lean R&D phases from the point of view of the team members. Indeed, the teams could use the approach to innovate and deliver value. Nevertheless, we identified opportunities for improvement concerning better supporting describing business hypotheses and providing clearer expectations on the activities conducted within each phase.

4.3 Lean R&D Acceptance

We elaborated statements on the perceived usefulness, ease of use, and behavioral intention to adopt Lean R&D based on the Technology Acceptance Model and asked participants to answer according to their agreement. The questionnaire was applied to the team members and the business and technical managers and sponsors of Petrobras and Americanas.

The results for the R&D team members can be seen in Fig. 4, while the results for the managers and sponsors of Petrobras can be seen in Fig. 5.

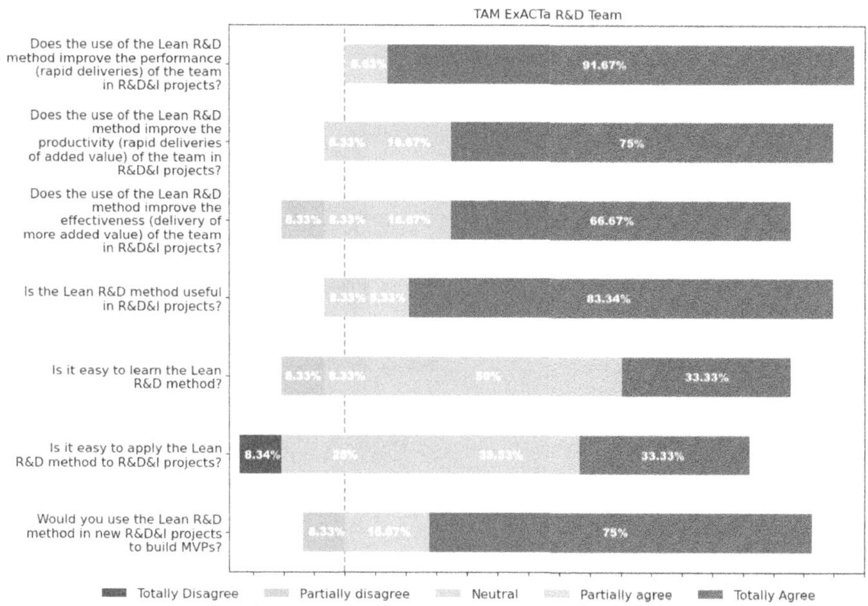

Fig. 4. Technology acceptance by the ExACTa R&D team members of the projects with Petrobras.

Analyzing Fig. 4, it is possible to observe a clear acceptance of Lean R&D among the R&D team members. Out of the twelve team members working with Petrobras, one partially disagreed on the improved effectiveness (added value) and the intention to use. This participant argued that the assessment of added value should receive more attention. Nevertheless, Lean R&D proposes continuous experimentation to measure the added value based on explicit business hypotheses. Another participant was skeptical about the ease of learning and applying Lean R&D, but provided no additional comments.

Based on Fig. 5, it is possible to understand that the managers and sponsors at Petrobras also had a large agreement. The only partial disagreement was of the sponsor and on the ease of use. In fact, he was only involved in the checkpoints.

The results for the ExACTa FIT team members can be seen in Fig. 6, while the results for the managers and sponsors of Americanas can be seen in Fig. 7.

Figure 6 shows that out of the 38 team members working with Americanas, just six partially or totally disagreed on any of the items. Only one of them commented, mentioning that applying the approach was not easy as they had

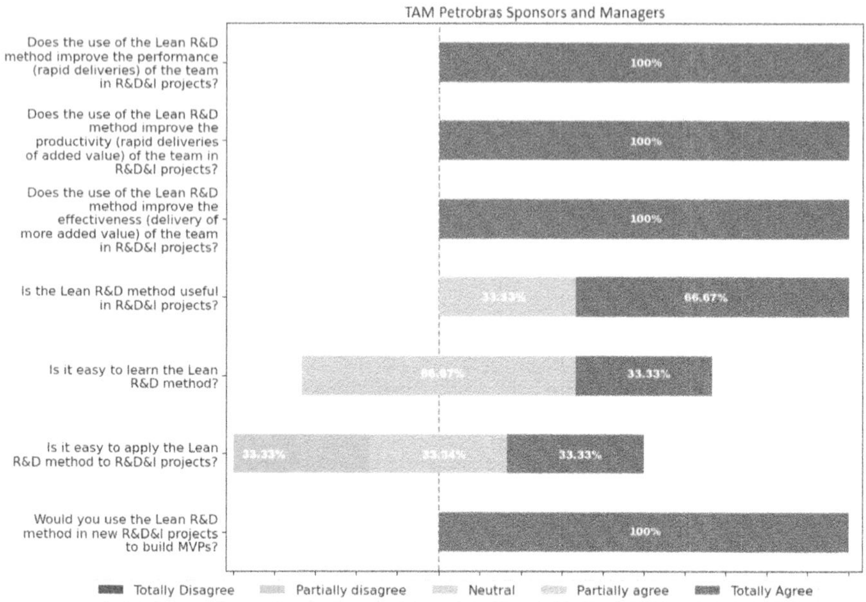

Fig. 5. Technology acceptance by the business and technical managers and sponsors of Petrobras.

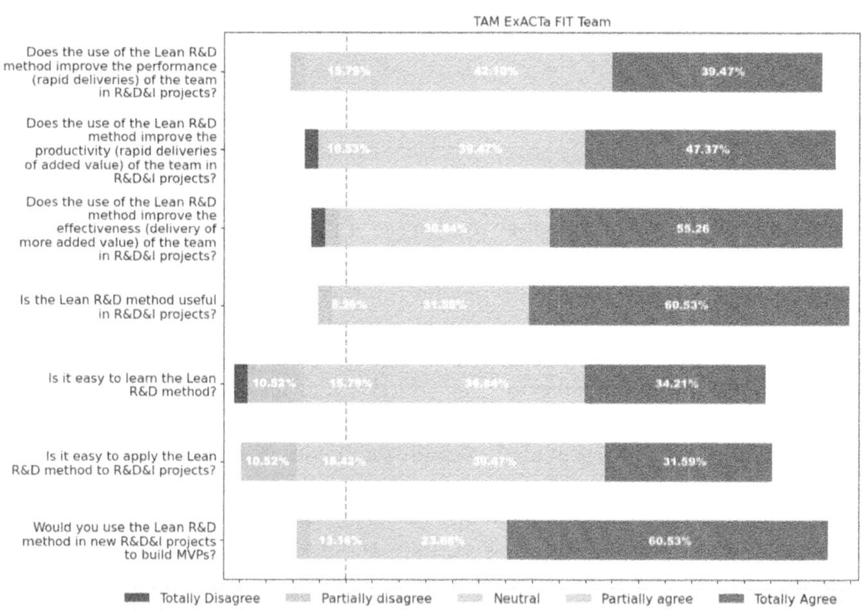

Fig. 6. Technology acceptance by the ExACTa FIT team members of the projects with Americanas.

limited prior experience. In fact, the most questioned statements concerned the ease of learning and applying Lean R&D. It is noteworthy that the team members were less experienced.

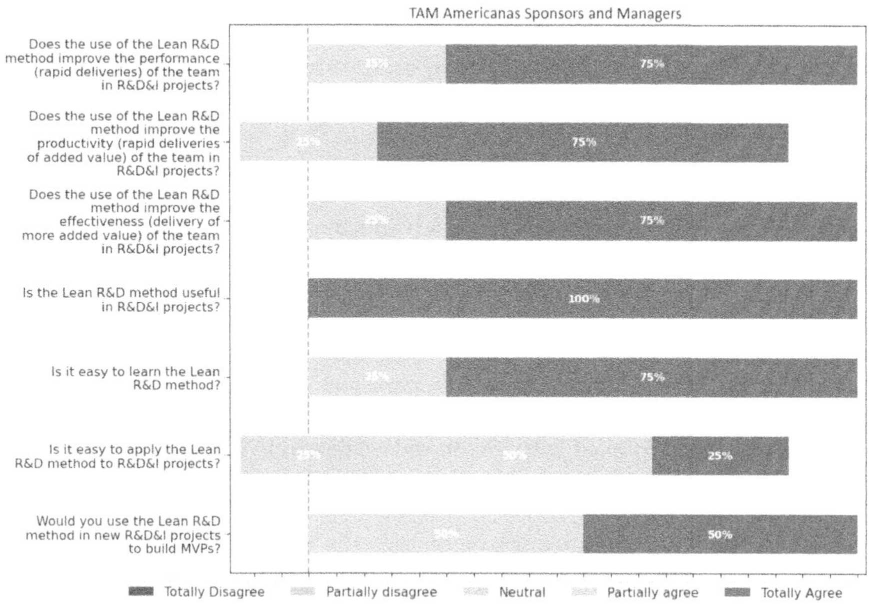

Fig. 7. Technology acceptance by the business and technical managers and sponsors of Americanas.

Figure 7 allows to observe that the managers and sponsors at Americanas also largely agreed with the TAM statements. One of the two managers more conservatively reported being neutral on the ease of use, and one of the two sponsors reported being neutral regarding improved productivity.

5 Discussion

The results from both the questionnaires and project outcomes reveal that Lean R&D was widely accepted by stakeholders at both Petrobras and Americanas, establishing its potential to meet a key success factor in IAC projects: achieving short-term, impactful results for industry. Stakeholders found Lean R&D's structure conducive to rapid iteration and tangible business outcomes, with many affirming the approach as suitable for aligning academic R&D efforts with pressing industry needs.

This compatibility highlights Lean R&D's utility in fulfilling the short-cycle demands of innovation projects, a benefit that distinguishes it from more traditional R&D frameworks, which often prioritize long-term objectives over immediate industry impact.

Another key factor contributing to Lean R&D's success in these projects was the iterative feedback loop between academic researchers and industry practitioners. This continuous feedback cycle allowed both parties to assess intermediate outcomes and make necessary adjustments, enhancing the relevance of the research outputs to address real-world issues effectively. This collaborative approach fostered an environment where theoretical knowledge and practical expertise could merge, enabling more accurate targeting of industry needs and ensuring that the academic efforts aligned closely with the company's innovation priorities.

However, these positive results should be viewed in light of other contributing factors that are critical to successful IACs [14]. The presence of collaboration champions on-site was particularly advantageous, as they provided essential project oversight and facilitated communication between academic and industry teams.

Additionally, strong support from company management and alignment with business strategy were crucial. Such backing allowed for smoother integration of academic R&D outputs into business operations, helping Lean R&D projects gain traction and relevancy within the company. A shared commitment to achieving industry results, coupled with an innovative research environment at the university, also played significant roles in supporting Lean R&D's acceptance and perceived effectiveness.

Further, the observed outcomes emphasize the adaptability of Lean R&D in different settings and its responsiveness to specific project requirements. In the case of Petrobras, the experienced R&D team leveraged Lean R&D to achieve measurable business outcomes in AI-driven projects, which led to international patent applications and prestigious awards.

Moreover, the Lean R&D approach's adaptability to evolving project scopes and changing business environments proved beneficial. With this respect, in both the Petrobras and Americanas projects, dynamic shifts in priorities due to market demands or organizational needs were seamlessly incorporated, demonstrating the approach's flexibility. This capacity to pivot and reprioritize based on real-time industry feedback ensured that the projects maintained their relevance and impact, further reinforcing Lean R&D's position as a practical methodology for driving meaningful collaboration in IAC projects.

This not only underscores Lean R&D's effectiveness in advancing sophisticated technological solutions but also demonstrates its value as a methodology capable of accelerating technology transfer from academia to industry. Petrobras's application of the MVP results in larger-scale development frameworks, like SAFe, further illustrates Lean R&D's complementary role in innovation pipelines.

For Americanas, involving less experienced students in Lean R&D projects provided a distinctive perspective on the approach's versatility. While some students highlighted challenges related to learning and applying the methodology, the majority affirmed Lean R&D's suitability and appreciated the opportunity to participate in every project phase, from ideation to MVP delivery. This empowered students to engage actively with real-world industry challenges, preparing them for future roles in R&D and fostering talent trained in the company's specific innovation context.

In summary, Lean R&D's ability to deliver impactful results in both short cycles and complex industry settings, combined with its strong acceptance among diverse stakeholder groups, positions it as a valuable framework for IAC projects. Nevertheless, the feedback received reveals opportunities for refinement, particularly in supporting the description of business hypotheses and clarifying the expectations around each phase's activities. By addressing these improvement areas, Lean R&D can further solidify its role in industry-academia collaborations to produce rapid and business-relevant results.

It should be noted that we report on experiences that, while valuable, inherently lack the scientific rigor associated with more systematic investigations. Specifically, the absence of a formal baseline or direct comparison to alternative frameworks, such as the Technology Transfer Model for co-production [3,4], limits the conclusions drawn about the effectiveness of Lean R&D in industry-academia collaboration. This shortcoming makes it challenging to contextualize the positive results and evaluate them relative to existing approaches.

6 Conclusion

Lean R&D has been used in IAC innovation projects of the ExACTa initiative with several industry partners. In this paper, we reported on recent results of applying the approach with Petrobras and Americanas, two large companies from the oil and gas and retail industry sectors.

In both experiences, the approach helped bring ideas to impactful business results. The projects delivered to Petrobras resulted in international patent applications and received a Petrobras inventor award at the end of 2022. Their ROI (calculated by the company and considering the investment in the R&D project against the yearly financial gains obtained from the solutions) exceeds the IAC investment by a factor of more than 1:20. With respect to Americanas, MVPs were successfully delivered in 2023, also positively impacting the business, as the company publicly acknowledged.

We also report perceptions on Lean R&D from the involved stakeholders. The assessment of the suitability of the phases pointed out that Lean R&D is perceived to help in defining a joined MVP vision, addressing research-related uncertainties early (in the technical feasibility phase), and efficiently delivering valuable MVPs. Furthermore, we observed the stakeholders' acceptance of the approach.

Opportunities for improvement include providing support for describing business hypotheses and clearly stating the expectations for activities conducted within each phase, making learning and applying the approach easier. Another opportunity one of the sponsors mentioned was more clearly defining the nature of the university collaboration with a greater focus on research, which could bring more innovative results.

Finally, we believe that sharing these experiences presents a valuable contribution to the community. In particular, the adaptability of Lean R&D across varying project scopes and company needs was evident, showcasing its potential to serve as a flexible methodology for different industry sectors. In the reported experiences both companies benefitted from Lean R&D's capacity to pivot in response to evolving project requirements and business priorities, ensuring relevance and maintaining momentum toward impactful results. This adaptability further emphasizes Lean R&D's strength as a framework for industry-academia collaboration, capable of aligning academic research efforts with dynamic industry landscapes to create practical, high-value outcomes.

References

1. Caroli, P.: Lean Inception: how to align people and build the right product. Editora Caroli (2018)
2. Fitzgerald, B., Stol, K.J.: Continuous software engineering: a roadmap and agenda. J. Syst. Softw. **123**, 176–189 (2017)
3. Gorschek, T., Garre, P., Larsson, S., Wohlin, C.: A model for technology transfer in practice. IEEE Softw. **23**(6), 88–95 (2006)
4. Gorschek, T., Mendez, D.: Solving problems or enabling problem-solving? from purity in empirical software engineering to effective co-production (invited keynote). In: Winkler, D., Biffl, S., Mendez, D., Wimmer, M., Bergsmann, J. (eds.) SWQD 2021. LNBIP, vol. 404, pp. 109–116. Springer, Cham (2021). https://doi.org/10.1007/978-3-030-65854-0_9
5. Kalinowski, M., et al.: Towards lean r&d: an agile research and development approach for digital transformation. In: 2020 46th Euromicro Conference on Software Engineering and Advanced Applications (SEAA), pp. 132–136. IEEE (2020)
6. Kalinowski, M., et al.: Lean r&d: an agile research and development approach for digital transformation. In: Product-Focused Software Process Improvement: 21st International Conference, PROFES 2020, Turin, Italy, 25–27 November 2020, Proceedings 21, pp. 106–124. Springer (2020). https://doi.org/10.1109/SEAA51224.2020.00030
7. Kuramoto, A.S.R., et al.: Method of assessment of the quality of the burn of the gases in the flare and adjustment to the vapor flow rate in a continuous and constant way (2023), uS Patent App. 17/890,539
8. Kuramoto, A.S.R., et al.: Method for detecting inaccuracies and gaps and for suggesting deterioration mechanisms and actions in inspection reports (2023), uS Patent App. 18/061,068
9. Monden, Y.: Toyota production system: an integrated approach to just-in-time. CRC Press (2011)
10. Ries, E.: The lean startup: How today's entrepreneurs use continuous innovation to create radically successful businesses. Crown Currency (2011)
11. Scaled Agile, Inc.: Scaled Agile Framework (SAFe). https://scaledagileframework.com/ (2023), Accessed 20 Jan 2025
12. Teixeira, B.R., et al.: Lessons learned from a lean r&d project. In: ICEIS, vol. (2), pp. 345–352 (2021)

13. Times Higher Education: Latin America University Rankings (2023). https://www.timeshighereducation.com/world-university-rankings/2023/latin-america-university-rankings (2023), Accessed August 2023
14. Wohlin, C., et al.: The success factors powering industry-academia collaboration. IEEE Softw. **29**(2), 67–73 (2011)

Author Index

J. Fischbach et al. (Eds.): SWQD 2025, LNBIP 544, p. 125, 2025.
https://doi.org/10.1007/978-3-031-89277-6

The manufacturer's authorised representative in the EU is Springer Nature Customer Service Centre GmbH, Europaplatz 3, 69115 Heidelberg, Germany. If you have any concerns regarding our products, please contact ProductSafety@springernature.com

Printed and bound by CPI Group (UK) Ltd, Croydon, CR0 4YY
30/09/2026
02225576-0008